£3

D1325546

BEHIND THE SCRUM

BEHIND
THE SCRUM
The Autobiography

Kyran Bracken

with Edward Griffiths

ORION

First published in hardback in Great Britain in 2004 by
Orion Books
an imprint of the Orion Publishing Group Ltd
Orion House, 5 Upper St Martin's Lane,
London WC2H 9EA

A CIP catalogue record for this book is available
from the British Library.

ISBN: 0 75286 844 6

Printed in Great Britain by
Butler and Tanner Ltd, Frome and London

Every effort has been made to fulfil requirements with regard to
reproducing copyright material. The author and publisher will be
glad to rectify any omissions at the earliest opportunity.

www.orionbooks.co.uk

CONTENTS

Dedication

This book is dedicated to my parents for starting the story, to my brother and sisters for continuing to follow the story, to my wife Victoria for the invaluable role she has played in the story . . . and to my young son, Charlie, so that one day he can read the story.

CHAPTER ONE

I am lying in bed, staring at two sleeping tablets on the table beside me. Should I take them or should I leave them? I need to sleep, but I don't want to rely on these. I'm not sure what to do.

The England team doctor usually gives these white pills to the players at the start of long-haul flights, but he also hands them out on the nights before major international matches. Most players take just one, but earlier this evening I asked the doctor to give me two because the last thing I want on the night before the Rugby World Cup final is a repeat of what happened to me before the home Test against South Africa in 2001.

I have struggled, for many years, to fall asleep, but that night was probably the worst. Back then, I took the sleeping pill at around eleven at night, only to lie there gazing at the ceiling until two o'clock in the morning. Then I got up, had a hot bath and hoped I would drift off while watching television. It didn't happen. By four in the morning, I was desperate. We were staying at the Pennyhill Park Hotel in Bagshot, Surrey, as usual, so I pulled on my tracksuit and set off to find the team doctor. He was pretty annoyed to be woken in the middle of the night, but he gave me another sleeping pill, told me to take another hot bath and sent me away.

In the end, I managed to get about three hours' sleep, instead of the eight hours most players would want, and that proved enough to get me through the match the following day. I played all right and we won 29–9, so there was no harm done.

The sleeping pills seemed to have helped, and I got used to taking them before major club matches as well as internationals. After a while I realised I didn't want to rely on them and so I stopped taking them in the summer of 2002. That's why I am lying here now, unsure of whether to take the tablets or not. I really want to sleep because tomorrow may well be the biggest match of my career, but I am scared of becoming dependent on these things.

It's all in the mind, people tell me. I know that. Of course it's in the mind. The problem is getting it out of my mind. Am I anxious about playing in the World Cup final? Of course I am. I feel the pressure like everyone else. I worry about making mistakes with so many millions of people watching on television. To be honest, since I contracted glandular fever in 1995 I've become much more anxious. That's when my problems started.

The doctor said it would be all right to continue playing rugby, even though I was suffering the typical tiredness associated with glandular fever; with hindsight, I know I should have taken a proper rest. I just didn't feel quite right. It was the kind of feeling you get with tonsillitis: your head is sore, your throat is dry and you have a sense of wanting to be sick. Come on, I used to tell myself, get a grip; and I would carry on, but everything seemed a real effort.

Nothing was as hard as sleeping, though.

I was getting only around three hours of sleep every night when I was recovering from glandular fever. I was battling to get to sleep and then waking really early in the morning, and week after week of that left me knackered. The symptoms persisted.

Eventually, early in 1997, I went to see a doctor specialising in what they call post-viral fatigue. He ran tests for recurrence of the glandular fever. When they came back negative, he started to investigate whether such a sustained period of sleeping badly had affected me in any way. He prescribed more pills and, for a few months, I felt and slept much better. So, through 1998, 1999 and 2000, I just about got by, getting maybe four hours' sleep each night but still managing to play pretty well and retain my place in the England squad.

Next, I started getting adrenaline rushes in the middle of the night. Just when I was trying to fall asleep, I would have that feeling you get before a big match: butterflies in the stomach, tension and a dryness in the mouth. It was bizarre. I tried all the usual remedies like taking a hot bath, drinking warm milk and reading a book, and these did calm me down a little, but I still couldn't sleep.

I arranged to see another specialist in London, and he raised the possibility that I was suffering from a condition where my throat kept closing during the night, and that was what woke me up. He asked me to undergo a sleep study to determine whether this was indeed the cause of all my problems. I was desperate to feel well, to sleep well and to be my old self again, so I agreed.

The sleep study was fixed to take place at a hospital, and I was shown to a room where the nurses carefully connected me to what felt like hundreds of different wires. Then, of course, I needed to go to the toilet, so I had to hobble along the corridor with all these wires attached to my body, aware of bystanders giggling at me.

When I finally settled, the staff told me to go to sleep, so they could start recording some readings. Easier said than done, I thought, and I was right. I found it hard enough falling asleep in my own bed, but it seemed impossible to sleep with these wires attached to me. So I just lay there. Everyone was growing frustrated. I eventually managed ten minutes' sleep and the doctors got some kind of reading, which showed I didn't suffer from the condition the specialist had suspected, but the exercise hadn't gone well. When I left the hospital that night, the nurses said I was the worst patient they had ever had.

At a follow-up appointment, the specialist told me there was nothing physically wrong, and that he reckoned my sleeping problems were all in the mind. That was the last thing I wanted to hear. It would have been easy if the problem could be neatly explained and treated with pills; instead, I was being left to contemplate the dark recesses of my mind.

Into 2001, my situation went from bad to worse. I started to feel sick more and more often, even when I was training. Anti-nausea tablets got me through the sessions, but I began to rely on everyday medication like Motilium. If that was not available, good old Rennies did the trick. At night I began taking Nytol, which helped, although within a few weeks I had started to believe I couldn't fall asleep without the tablets.

Still the nausea persisted. It drove me to see yet another specialist. He asked some questions, felt around and then said he wanted to put a tube down my throat, to check my stomach and take a sample of the lining for analysis. I eagerly agreed, and condemned myself to what turned out to be, by some margin, the most unpleasant experience of my life so far.

'Would you like to be sedated?' the nurse asked.

'No, thanks,' I replied, bristling with rugby machismo. 'I have to drive home afterwards, so I'll be fine.'

This was a mistake. I lay on the bed while a thick tube was pushed down the back of my throat. The nurse kept telling me to gulp as I felt this thing go deeper and deeper into my stomach. I retched, but there was nothing inside. Every five seconds or so for at least ten minutes, I started to writhe and felt as though I was going to be sick. It was absolute hell.

My intense pain was not in vain, however, because the analysis revealed a bug called *Helicobacter*, an organism that eats away at the lining of your stomach, causing ulcers that can become cancerous. At last, I thought, we are getting somewhere. The doctor prescribed more pills, which wiped out the bug, and I began to look forward to a normal life again, free from stomach pains.

The optimism didn't last. Within a week, I seemed to be back at square one, feeling nauseous again. I reverted to my old friends, the Motilium and the Rennies, and struggled on.

Matches came and went. I was playing pretty well, both for Saracens and England. Strangely, somehow, I don't think anyone outside my closest family and friends realised what I was going through. To the outside world, I was a successful professional rugby player having a great time.

The nausea became severe during half time of the Six

Nations international against Ireland at Twickenham in February 2002. Everything was going OK. We were winning well, and I was having a decent game at scrum-half, but as soon as I reached the changing room I felt this sudden urge to be sick and I spent the entire interval retching violently in the toilet. This kind of reaction is not particularly unusual in international rugby – players show the tension in different ways – but it was unusual for me. Combined with everything else, it seemed to confirm that something still wasn't completely right.

Soon I was getting adrenaline rushes during the day as well as at night, and they started to be followed by a splitting headache – a searing burst of pain in my temples every time I felt the rush start to pulse through my stomach. Bloody hell, I was a mess.

Lack of sleep, constant nausea, repeated adrenaline rushes and shattering headaches: this was my life in the spring of 2002. I kept up appearances but, inside, I was frustrated. I had seen three specialists and seemed to have got nowhere.

What now?

'Hello, Simon, it's Kyran Bracken.'

'Hi, how can I help?'

I had decided to call Simon Kemp, the England team doctor, and he was brilliant. He listened to my entire story, and seemed to understand exactly what I was going through. Honest enough to say he didn't think there was anything he could do, he then suggested I should contact a sports psychologist. Simon gave me the telephone number of Britt Tajet-Foxell, from Denmark, working in London, and, without sounding dramatic about everything, she started to change my life.

Through a series of consultations, she made me understand that I was suffering from anxiety and that it was manifesting itself in various physical symptoms. She helped me take stock of my life, and she explained how my thought processes over the past seven years had caused the difficulties. We broke down my thinking and, together, began to change the way I was interpreting my thoughts. She showed me breathing techniques to counter adrenaline rushes, and she taught me how to relax and how to cope with the pressure.

'Change the way you think,' Britt told me again and again, 'and you will eventually change the way you feel.'

By the end of 2002, our progress was such that I was starting to sleep much better. I still suffered anxiety, but Britt had taught me how to control it and how to ensure it didn't control me.

So here I am, lying in bed at the England team hotel on the eve of the Rugby World Cup final against Australia, and it's now well past eleven o'clock and I'm still staring at the sleeping tablets on the table. And I have decided I'm *not* going to take them. I won't have any problems sleeping tonight. I'll be fine.

Come on, Kyran, I tell myself, you're about to be involved in a World Cup final. Stop worrying. You feel fine. The World Cup final is a few hours away. I can hardly believe this is happening to me, can hardly believe I have this opportunity. Just think, I tell myself, how far you've come to get to this time and place ...

At the start of 2003, it had seemed I was just about as far away from the England squad as it was possible to be. Matt Dawson had played in the autumn internationals of 2002 and apparently taken possession of the scrum-half's position ahead of World Cup year. Gloucester's Andy Gomarsall appeared to be the nominated reserve. I was past thirty-one and generally reckoned to be drifting over the hill.

Even so, ten years into a rollercoaster England career, I wasn't going to give up easily. Ever since my debut against New Zealand in 1993, I had generally been included in the squad and always seemed in contention, but I had been in and out of the starting XV more times than I could remember. In rugby, I had learned to expect the unexpected and always to be prepared.

So it happened. I was chosen to captain England A against France, but withdrew because I had been concussed in a club match the week before and was not fully recovered. The next day, I heard Dawson had been injured and had pulled out of the England team to play France in the Six Nations. Gomarsall was going to start and Nick Walshe had been called up as the substitute.

I was annoyed. Maybe that was my chance, and I had blown it. If I had not withdrawn from the A side, I would have been on the England bench, back in the squad and in with a chance. Instead, I had been cautious and would be watching the match on TV.

The game didn't go well for England, but the guys scrambled a win. The next week, relaxing in a pub with my wife, Victoria, and still feeling upset about missing my golden chance, the name 'Clive Woodward' suddenly flashed up on my mobile.

'KB,' he said, 'I want you to play against Wales.'

The coach said he wasn't happy with Gommers, which was his prerogative. He thought he had kicked away too much ball and, as I knew only too well, once Clive gets an idea in his head, it stays there. I was shocked. I thought Andy had done quite well.

Without even finishing the half-pint, I walked home with my arm around Victoria and immediately called my parents and my brother, John, to tell them the news. They were thrilled for me, and said the recall was exactly what I deserved. I wasn't so sure. Sport can be very strange. When you think you're playing really well, nobody notices but, now, when my form for Saracens had been OK but not sparkling, I was suddenly being catapulted right back into the England team.

Quietly, privately, I wondered whether I still had what it takes to perform at the highest level. I had genuinely not expected to get this opportunity, and I started to feel uneasy again. I phoned Britt, and she talked me through some breathing techniques and told me to focus on positive think-ing. That helped, and Victoria spent hours with me, filling me with confidence and self-belief.

The newspapers were calling me 'Lazarus' and the 'Come-back King', which amused me, and by the time the squad assembled in Cardiff I felt everything was just about under control.

As the first training session started, the pressure built up inside me. Ten years of international experience seemed to count for nothing, and I felt as if it was my first cap I was preparing to win against Wales at the Millennium Stadium on Saturday. Some of the players were ribbing me, picking up on the Lazarus tag, but I gave as good as I got. To them, I was the same old bright and breezy KB.

In fact, I was worried about the calls. They had all changed since I was last in the squad and, playing in the pivotal position of scrum-half, it was vital that I knew them by heart. Nothing seemed to be sinking in, so when we were given a day off and most of the guys went to play golf, I drove back to Hertfordshire so I could spend some time at home and get my head right.

Victoria was there for me again, and she spent more than two hours testing me on the calls, asking me over and over again until I had everything clear in my mind. Even then I wasn't satisfied, and I went down to the Saracens training ground in Southgate where, on my own, I walked up and down the field, going through the calls.

All the time, I was working so hard to keep everything under control. When I was young, I went out and played and had a great time and loved every minute, but as I have grown older it has become more difficult to deal with the pressure. Surely it should have been the other way around? I don't know. Anyway, it was hard work trying to keep on top of the situation.

I arrived back at the team hotel just after eight o'clock in the evening, and happened to meet Jason Robinson in the lift.

'Do you get nervous?' I asked him out of the blue.

'Not really,' he said, smiling.

I envied him. Maybe our full-back just had so much confidence in his own ability that he didn't worry about anything. As I walked back to my room, I thought how great it would be if you could buy that kind of self-belief in a shop. I wished I could feel like Jason. Maybe it's all in your genes. My mum gets the yips when she plays golf, so perhaps I get the worrying from her.

The preparations went well and, as always in Cardiff, there was a wonderful atmosphere in the build-up to the game. Welsh people are not generally the biggest fans of the

England rugby team and wherever we went in town people either swore at us or just flicked V-signs in our direction. Most of us were used to it and weren't fazed at all. In fact, we really enjoyed the banter.

Our training session on the Friday afternoon gave me my first sight of the Millennium Stadium, and I was impressed by its sheer size and the quality of the playing surface. As I looked around at the rows of seats, I felt the pressure mounting again. Just at that moment, Jonny Wilkinson was practising his punting. Right foot, left foot: it made no difference as, again and again, the ball soared unerringly towards the touchline. He's so good, I thought to myself, and quickly began to feel calm.

All went well. I even got seven hours' sleep the night before the game, without taking any sleeping pills, and I felt a huge sense of pride as we sang 'God Save the Queen'. After being so far away, it was good to be back in the thick of things.

The game went well. I made all my tackles and hit each of my passing targets. I wish I could have focused on those positives but, unfortunately, that's not my nature. Early in the first half, a Welsh forward had come through a ruck offside and knocked the ball out of my hands. The referee gave the knock-on against me. A similar thing happened in the second half, and I was upset because I knew these two 'mistakes' would be marked down by the coaching staff and would count against me. Dawson was going to be fit again soon, and I needed to be perfect to keep my place.

I also had a run-in with Martin Johnson. At a line-out, I called the captain to loop round after the next ruck. When it happened, he wasn't there and at the next line-out I went mad, shouting at him to wake up and concentrate on what he was doing. To be honest, I wasn't completely sure I had made the right call, but I backed myself and blazed away at Johnno. He was taken aback and, as I kept swearing, he looked at me blankly. I started to worry that I had made a terrible mistake but when the final whistle went a few minutes later, confirming our hard-fought 26–9 victory, Johnno came up to me and said: 'Well bossed.'

So I presume I did the right thing. I felt good about the way I had played, at least until I heard about Jeremy Guscott slagging me off on television for the two knock-ons. It's especially hard when people you consider to be your friends criticise you, but I'm sure Jerry didn't mean it personally. I'm just the sensitive type and, as always, Victoria took the brunt of my irritation, having to spend the next forty-eight hours hearing me moan about offside flankers.

It turned out Clive Woodward agreed with the critics. Dawson was recalled for the following Six Nations match, against Italy at Twickenham, and I was sent back to the bench, though I actually got on as a second-half substitute in that game, on the wing.

The rollercoaster soars, and plunges. One day, I was thrilled by my comeback. The next, I was in despair, right back where I had started. Clive phoned and said he wanted to rotate Gommers and me on the bench and so had put me back in the A side for the match against Scotland. I thought it was unfair, and told him that if I did well I wanted to be involved in the next Six Nations game.

Anger is a great motivator. I captained the A side to a record win over the Scots, scored a try and, in my opinion at least, ran the show. I was so pumped after the game that I did something I had never done before in my entire career. I called Clive's mobile and left a message saying I wanted my place back. Eventually, he replied with a message to say I would be in the squad for the Six Nations decider against Ireland in Dublin. The rollercoaster was soaring again. So it goes in professional sport.

The preparations for Dublin were intense. Nobody involved in the England squad needed to be reminded that we had blown Grand Slam deciders in 2000, 2001 and 2002 – even though the papers did exactly that every day of the week – and we were seriously resolved not to slip up again in 2003. Clive was very matter-of-fact about everything. He decided we would remain in England until three days before the match, helping the players to stay more relaxed. I certainly appreciated the chance to go home now and then to spend time with Victoria. I was feeling fine, staying confident, getting ready to play.

As usual, the management produced a video montage at the team meeting on the night before the match, and this time they had edited a selection of big hits, tries and glory shots to the Eminem song 'Lose Yourself' with its theme of 'One shot, one opportunity'. The video struck a chord with the players, and Clive stressed the point, saying we had one chance to win the Grand Slam. They may have made an unlikely pair, but Eminem and Clive combined to implant the message in our minds: there were going to be no excuses for failure.

On the afternoon of the match at Lansdowne Road, I knew for certain we were going to win when, even before a ball had been kicked, I witnessed the most outstanding, brilliant piece of leadership.

We had run onto the field first and, amid a cacophony of Irish booing and excitement, Johnno led us to line up to the right of the halfway line, as you see it from the main stand, ready for the national anthems to be played. There was a long red carpet laid out in front of us, for the dignitaries to use when they were introduced to the players, and everything seemed fine.

Then an agitated Irish official approached Johnno and asked him if he would take the England team to the opposite side of the halfway line. He said something about the right-hand side being traditionally lucky for the Ireland team. Johnno gave this guy the evil eye and unequivocally told him to 'piss off'.

'We're not moving for anybody,' the England captain said. 'We are starting this end, and if Ireland want to stand on our left, they're welcome to **** off past the red carpet.'

As the official scurried away, the crowd began to realise what was happening and they started to boo. Johnno just stood there, his chest out, unmovable, every inch the genuinely great England rugby captain that history will surely judge him to be. Eventually, the Irish reluctantly lined up on the other side. Johnno had made it abundantly clear to everyone that we were there to win and we were not going to let anybody mess us around. It was a great moment, and confidence rippled through our side.

We started well, silenced the crowd within twenty minutes and had the game in our pocket soon after half time. I managed to get on the field twice during the second half, first when Dawson needed treatment after cutting his nose open, then again near the end. Part of the crowd saw me as a traitor, playing for England despite my Irish background, and they booed when I ran on. I didn't mind, but things began to get dangerous when the spectators started throwing coins at the England substitutes. A few years ago, Austin Healey had made a joke of a similar situation by running around to collect the coins and put them in his pocket, but some of the missiles were landing too close for comfort. It was a bit disappointing because the Irish crowd is generally one of the fairest and most entertaining in the world.

Anyway, we won the game 42–6 and emphatically claimed the Grand Slam. The guys were delighted, and we set off on a lap of honour with the cup and our medals. Later we were spraying champagne around the dressing room and having a great time. Pressure? What pressure? Right then, it seemed a million miles away.

Clive Woodward stood apart. When someone shouted for him to pose for a photograph, holding the Six Nations trophy with his management team, he initially declined and was only reluctantly persuaded to stand to one side. My mind flashed back to similar scenes in 1995, when England won the Grand Slam and the then coach, Jack Rowell, made sure he was right in the middle of all the celebrations. Clive was very different.

As soon as we had changed and returned to the hotel, he called a team meeting. 'Good teams win Grand Slams,' the coach said, 'but great teams win World Cups. All we are tonight is a good team. To be a great team, we have to step up a gear and become World Champions, and that will take a huge effort. Enjoy the evening, but keep what I have said in the back of your mind.'

A sugar-coated version of events would then relate how the room fell quiet, and the players nodded sagely. In reality, life is not so sweet, and a few people complained that Clive was taking away the glory. Someone muttered the word 'killjoy'. Deep down, we all knew Clive was right but, that particular night, everyone wanted a big night out. Over the years, I have learned that it's important to celebrate your victories because your next defeat is generally just around the corner. You have to enjoy the good times.

After the official dinner, we headed for Leeson Street, popping in and out of bars. Jason Leonard knew the right spots to go, so most of us followed him. We ended up in a nightclub with the Irish players, and the night got messy. Such parties, with both teams getting plastered together long into the night, have always been one of the best things about rugby. Sadly, it happens all too rarely under the modern regime of optimum fitness, healthy diets and so on.

The England squad travelled home with hangovers and, just a couple of weeks later, each of us received a special souvenir of our 2003 Six Nations Grand Slam: all five match programmes from the campaign displayed with photos in a frame. Clive had hand-written a personal inscription on each montage, always finishing with the question 'Can we now go from good to great?' He was laying it on thick, but he wanted to get his message across: the Six Nations was fine, but it was the World Cup that really mattered.

Nobody was really looking forward to the summer tour of 2003 and the away Tests against New Zealand and Australia. Most of us were exhausted at the end of a long, gruelling season, and would far rather have headed for a sunny beach.

Touring used to be one of the top experiences for any player. It used to be all about seeing a new country, meeting new people, playing some good rugby and drinking lots and lots. Unfortunately, in the professional era, that has all changed. Nowadays, touring is about seeing a hotel room, meeting the coaching staff for a one-on-one analysis of your performance and training lots and lots.

Of course the players must be professional in their approach and responsible in their preparations. We are well paid and obliged to give value for money. I completely accept that. But there should be a middle way, where rugby can still be rugby, where every now and then the players can be human, not robots. The grim realities of a professional tour are a general ban on drinking, an insistence on proper recovery time, detailed analysis of every match followed by refocusing on the next game ... drone ... drone ... drone ... drone. No wonder the guys couldn't wait to get home.

I should count myself lucky to have been involved in some great tours before the legions of oh-so-serious management gurus and technical specialists invaded our sport. Back in those days we had a wobble wig for the biggest moaner in the squad, and special court sessions to deal with offences during the tour. There was always a Fines Committee, maintaining discipline, and a Social Committee, seeking out the best places to visit. These have all gone. In the pro game, we're lucky to get a round of golf, tops.

Still, that's the job and we have to get on with it. So at the end of May 2003 the England squad gathered again and we began to 'refocus' on the southern-hemisphere tour. The media described the exercise as preparation for the World Cup later in the year but, as players, we didn't see the tour in such terms. We were tired, and just wanted to get it done so that we could have some rest.

In sport, it often seems as though the management and press try to hype up every tournament and tour as some kind of grand and noble mission, when the less glamorous reality is a group of players simply trying to survive and keep their places. They talk about records and glory; we talk about mortgages.

That doesn't mean we didn't want to win: we were desperate to win every game. Or that we didn't train hard: we gave 100 per cent in every practice session. As players, we were just a bit more gritty and realistic about what we were doing. The phenomenon is hardly new. In the England team, as in the English army at Agincourt, we were the foot soldiers, occasionally grumbling about the preening generals, but working hard to win the battle.

Personally, I should have been feeling reasonably confident about my own position. I appeared to have secured my place in the squad during the Six Nations, and was part of everything. In fact, I was getting restless again. Gomarsall was playing well for his club, Gloucester, and he was buzzing. I felt the pressure. There were three scrum-halves included in the tour party, but I wanted to be one of the top two, starting or at least in the Test squad.

We arrived in New Zealand and I was put in the starting XV for the opening match of the tour, against the traditionally formidable NZ Maori team, with Gommers on the bench. We were separated from the rest of the squad to prepare for the game, and the training went well, although I was constantly aware of my rival being keen and enthusiastic, looking sharp and in form. The better he looked, the more I knew I had to perform.

Similar situations in the past have had me nervously watching the coach, looking for any indication of approval or hostility, any sign of whether I was in or out of favour, but it was never like that with Clive. He always let you know exactly where you stood, and the players respected him for that.

We had been told that Clive and his assistant coach, Andy Robinson, wanted to sit down with each of the players individually at some stage of the tour, and these sessions would be arranged in alphabetical order. 'B' for Bracken put me at the front of the queue, and I was called to see them two days before the match against the Maoris. True to form, the coach was blunt.

'This is how I see the scrum-half situation,' Clive said. 'You're far behind Matt (Dawson), and on a par with Gommers. Honestly, I don't have a dilemma picking my first choice any more, KB. As you know, you have often been my first choice in the past but, after the Six Nations campaign, Matt is now my scrum-half.'

I nodded. I didn't particularly like what he said, but it was fair enough and I certainly wasn't going to argue.

Clive continued: 'I hope you realise the importance of this game against the Maoris for you personally. It may well be the most important match of your career. Your World Cup place is on the line and you need a fantastic game to be part of my plans.'

'OK,' I replied. 'Thanks, Clive.'

And I had been feeling worried before the meeting!

I walked straight to my hotel room and phoned Victoria. She was brilliant, telling me not to worry about what Clive had said and just to play the game. I also called my brother, John, and he said the coaches were playing mind games, because they would have to take three scrum-halves to the World Cup and there was nobody pushing Matt, Gommers and me. He said I would be OK.

Just to maintain my confidence, I telephoned Britt back in London, and she tried to talk me through some visualisation techniques, but it didn't really work because I couldn't relax. It was hard for me to focus on anything apart from the game, the pressure of having to perform, the World Cup, everything.

On the day of the Maoris match, each of us in the team was called to a one-on-one meeting with Andy Robinson. I was scheduled to meet Robbo for ten minutes, but stayed more than an hour. There was history between us, and some things needed to be said.

I walked into his room and, before he could say a word, told him exactly what was on my mind. 'Look, Robbo,' I said. 'I know you are my stumbling block. You're the reason I don't get picked for England, because you don't rate me. Well, I disagree. I think I am the best scrum-half, and I'll prove that tonight.'

He looked a bit dumbfounded, but I felt a whole lot better. I had complete respect for Andy's technical knowledge – he knows the game well – but I didn't appreciate his niggling, critical approach at training. His big idea was to rub players up the wrong way in the hope of getting a reaction, so he would frequently rip into Lawrence Dallaglio at practice, and he generally seemed to be getting on the back of Danny Grewcock and Julian White – and me. The guys called him 'Growler' because he often growled at people and he frequently put on his 'mean' face when he spoke to you.

In 2001, the day before the autumn international against the Wallabies at Twickenham, Robbo had come up to me aggressively and asked me: 'Are you up to it?' Before I could ask him what the hell he was talking about, he turned and walked away.

Whoopee! That was really going to motivate me. Andy had played most of his career under Jack Rowell at Bath, and he seemed to be a disciple of the former England coach. 'Be critical, ask searching questions and the players will respond,' they reckoned. I didn't agree.

The assistant coach had also annoyed me on a couple of

occasions when I was actually in the starting XV and Matt was on the bench but Robbo still asked my rival for his opinion on a technical aspect of what we were doing. I liked Daws a lot, and didn't want to be sensitive, but it was hard not to feel undermined when my understudy was telling the team what to do.

To be fair, Robbo took what I said on board, explained why he was a fan of Jack Rowell and his methods, and then constructively suggested we should talk about why he didn't particularly rate me. It came down to his opinion that I didn't control the forwards at the breakdown point, especially at rucks. He said my calls to pick and go were not effective, and I knew that Matt had a special talent for opening holes in the middle of rucks. He made a reasonable case, and I understood his point of view, although I did wonder why he hadn't found the time to say anything to me before.

We had an evening kick-off against the Maoris. I don't enjoy night games because it always seems such a long wait and the day drags on and on. Most of the guys have a sleep during the afternoon but, needless to say, my nerves always keep me awake. It's difficult enough for me to fall asleep at two o'clock in the morning, let alone two o'clock in the afternoon. So I lay on my bed and thought about the game and its importance. Maybe I thought too much.

It began to rain while we were in the bus and by the time we reached the stadium the rain was really lashing down. When we looked out from the players' tunnel, visibility was down to less than fifteen yards. This was all I needed. I always hate playing in the wet because the ball gets slippery and difficult to pass.

As I walked back to the changing room, the pressure of the

situation hit home. I was mindful of what Clive had said, concerned about the weather and determined to perform. I had to work hard to hold everything together and keep my poise.

What studs should I use? I wasn't sure. I thought about using some football studs that I had in my bag. Then I decided to wear longer rugby studs and threw the football studs into the plastic rubbish bin. I don't know why I did that. I just did it. When we went out to warm up in the rain, the studs felt really uncomfortable and I thought I needed the football studs after all.

They were now in the bin. So, in front of everyone, I turned it upside down, emptied the rubbish and slowly picked out the football studs, one by one. Robbo looked at me as though I was crazy, but I wanted those studs and I didn't care how I looked or what anyone thought. If I get an idea in my head, it stays there. After a while, I had found them all except one and used a rugby stud to make up the full set. The situation had got me flustered.

Kick-off seemed to settle me down and I played with what I can only describe as raw commitment. I was constantly screaming instructions to the forwards, and things seemed to go well in what was an intense, physical match. We were safely in the lead midway through the second half, and I felt pleased when they took me off to give Gomarsall a run. Job done, I thought.

Life is rarely so simple. Within five minutes, Gommers made a brilliant sixty-yard break and scored a try from the resulting scrum. In these situations, players are meant to be happy for their rival, but I felt sick. It looked like game, set and match to him.

Back at the hotel, I phoned Victoria, John and my parents.

They all felt I had played well but everyone shared my concern over Gommers' storming performance. Oh well, I concluded, there's not much I can do about that. I'll just wait and see.

The management verdict turned out to be more positive than I had expected. They were pleased with the way I had directed the pack and it emerged that, even from their seats high in the stands, they had been able to hear me calling 'Pick! Pick! Pick!' to the forwards, urging them to take it forward. In their eyes, I had done what they asked and controlled the game, so I was named on the bench for the Test match against New Zealand.

My confidence grew, and I eased through a calm week. Clive was keen for us to get as much rest as possible, so training was light in the mornings and the guys typically spent the rest of the days sitting and chatting in coffee shops near our hotel.

I spent one amazing afternoon with Jason Robinson and Jamie Noon. Over coffee, we somehow got onto the subject of religion and Jason talked openly about his days of drinking and partying. He explained how everything changed when he met Va'aiga Tuigamala, the All Black wing, at Wigan, and told how his life had become much more fulfilling ever since he had become a Christian. My instinct is to be wary of the God Squad, so Noony and I pestered Jason with questions all afternoon and his responses were absolutely brilliant. Then, when we spoke about our own beliefs, or lack of them, he was genuinely interested and sympathetic. As we walked back to the hotel, I still didn't know what I believed in, but I had enjoyed talking to Jason about his faith.

Expect the unexpected. Just as I was congratulating myself

on securing a place on the bench, I heard Dawson was injured and had been forced to withdraw. Within the space of seventy-two hours, I had moved from the brink of ignominy in my chat with Clive and Robbo to being back in the England No. 9 jersey.

The news provoked the same double-edged reaction as usual. I was delighted to be back in the team because that is where I felt I belonged, but it also brought back the pressure. I hadn't felt too well since leaving England but, as the All Black Test approached, I began to suffer tiredness. I didn't have energy for anything and the training sessions became a real struggle.

On the night before the Test, I spent some time sitting on the floor of the corridor outside my hotel room, talking to my brother on the telephone. I told him exactly how I was feeling and, as always, he was sympathetic and understanding. 'Nobody knows that you're feeling knackered,' he said. 'It doesn't show on TV. You look good, so just pretend you're fine and get on with it.'

New Zealand is nothing if not a rugby country, and the city of Wellington was buzzing on the day of the international. It seemed as if everyone we met, from the hotel staff to people working in any shop we visited, was fully aware of who we were, why we were in their country and how the All Blacks would win.

However, where we found V-signs in Cardiff, there were only admiring glances in the capital city of New Zealand. As usual, on the morning of the Test we went to practise our line-out drills in a park near our hotel and, while we ran around, a reasonable-sized crowd just seemed to materialise out of nothing. They were respectful, in awe of the big names like Johnno and Jonny, and they appeared to enjoy the spectacle. I know some New Zealanders feel this incredible level of public interest often puts too much pressure on the All Blacks but, deep down, they wouldn't have it any other way. It's a great rugby country.

I felt surprisingly calm on the day, maybe because I have always played well against the All Blacks. It's odd how perceptions like that stick with a player and make a real difference. Even when the wind started to blow and it began to rain, I was still confident and cheerful. Everything was going to be OK.

The match was a cracker, tough and intense. I was going well and managed to catch All Black scrum-half Justin Marshall twice, both times on his pass at the base of the scrum. They squandered a couple of chances, Jonny kicked his goals, Carlos Spencer didn't and we were clinging to a 15–13 lead with time running out.

The Test had turned on one scrum, which had been set when we had only thirteen players on the field. With two of our forwards in the sin-bin, we were looking a bit ragged and the All Blacks were hunting for what would almost certainly be a winning score. As I prepared to feed the ball, I sensed they fancied their chances against our weakened pack.

In fact, our props, Phil Vickery and Graham Rowntree, dug their studs into the turf and stood firm. It was an amazing feat, and we kept the ball. I felt fantastic after the game, not least because I had played the full eighty minutes and done well. That night, I lay awake in bed and wondered whether my performance would be enough to keep my place in the starting XV. Daws was clearly going to be fit for the Test against Australia on Saturday, but I still thought I might have done enough.

Anyway, it was out of my hands. I got a good press in New Zealand, where the papers credited me with disrupting the base of the All Black scrum, but it was Clive's opinion that mattered. It was only after a couple of days in Melbourne that he announced his team to play the Wallabies. I was there at No. 9, holding my place and apparently the man in possession once again. I didn't have to imagine how Matt was feeling because I knew.

The Australian media responded to our arrival with the usual volleys of Pom-bashing and hype. They could hardly wait to remind us of the historical blip that England had played ten Tests against the Wallabies in Australia, and never won. We hardly needed extra motivation, but it was accepted none the less.

Then they tried to embroil us in a controversy over whether the large sliding roof of the Colonial Stadium, the Test venue, should be left open to the elements or closed. Describing us as 'wet weather' specialists, they maintained that a decision to shut the roof and keep out the forecast rain would benefit Australia.

I suppose there was a time when England touring squads may have been distracted by such prattle, but we were too experienced to take any notice. Clive took the wind out of their sails by declaring he, too, would like the roof closed for the Test, adding that England would also prefer to play on a dry, hard field.

We trained at the stadium on the day before the match, and I really enjoyed the perfect conditions. It felt as though I was back at school, playing in a sports hall. Our voices echoed around the empty stadium but, with the roof closed, the venue felt a bit like an oven. It was boiling hot and, as we jogged around, we began peeling off layers to keep cool.

As we practised, we noticed people putting large gold cards on each seat in the stadium. When the Lions had played there in 2001, the red colours had apparently outnumbered the gold in the stadium, and the Aussies clearly didn't want a repeat of that situation, so they were leaving nothing to chance.

I was feeling OK. One minute I was bouncing around, pleased to be part of the team again, in the middle of everything, shouting out calls, feeling in control; the next moment, during a break in training at the Dome, I gazed across the rows and rows of empty seats and visualised thousands of people watching the Test, wanting me to make a mistake and fail. This was what playing for England always meant to me: it was pride and pressure.

Come on, I told myself, stay positive; and I did. I made the usual phone calls to my wife, my brother and my parents, got to sleep that night, kept calm through the day and managed to play my part in another bold, efficient England performance.

We were leading by half time, but playing indoors had been harder than any of us imagined. Everyone was sweating profusely and battling to drink enough fluids. I felt particularly tired and didn't know how I was going to get through the second half. In the event, I didn't have to. Clive substituted me, to bring on Matt in the fifty-eighth minute and I watched the rest of the Test from the bench.

At first I thought I had played pretty well, but as I sat there I worried whether I had done enough. Did Clive feel Matt would lift the team? Was that why he had taken me off? I thought back over the game and, inevitably, settled on a couple of mistakes. Ever the perfectionist, I was giving myself a hard time again, focusing on a few incidents, blowing them out of all proportion in my own mind, internalising the criticism and getting restless.

Ben Cohen scored a fantastic try to seal our 25–14 win, but by then I had successfully managed to convince myself that I had not played well enough to stay on the park and that I had wasted my chance again. I celebrated with the rest of the guys in the changing room – back-to-back wins against New Zealand and Australia was a great achievement, especially only four months before we returned for the World Cup – but, for me, I don't know . . . perhaps I did play well. Maybe I was just being negative. I hope so.

In fact, nobody went overboard that night. We just wanted to get home and start the summer break, and there was a fair amount of irritation among the players that, instead of leaving for London the next morning, we were having to pack for Perth. It was Clive's idea that at the end of the summer tour we should spend an extra three days getting to know the environment, the stadium and the city that would be our base for the first two matches of our 2003 Rugby World Cup campaign. The coach's logic was faultless, as usual, but the guys were mentally on the beach. So we sat at Melbourne airport and moaned and speculated how much we would pay for the right to get on the direct flight back to London. The consensus was that we would hand back all our appearance money just to go home.

Clive overlooked the grumbling and kept his focus, and we soon realised his three-day exercise had been planned like a military operation. We stayed in the same hotel, visited the stadium and even took a video of the changing room at precisely the same time of day that we would play our opening match. Eventually, even the grumpiest among us had to concede the visit had been worthwhile, but that didn't stop us from extracting some measure of compensation by spending each evening at a top restaurant and sending the bill back to the RFU.

Not everything went according to plan, however. After dinner on the first night, we had trouble finding a bar that was open. Everyone was getting increasingly irritated, so when we finally saw a place, a large group of us piled in and ordered a round of drinks. After a few minutes, it dawned on us that it was a gay venue. Guys were snogging each other on the dance floor, and the women looked quite butch.

We decided we would finish our drinks and then leave, but the atmosphere between the strapping, muscular England rugby team and the regular clientele of the gay bar was interesting to say the least. If anyone had taken a photograph and sent it to an Australian newspaper, we would never have lived it down.

One of the locals then approached Josh Lewsey on his way to the toilet, made some kind of provocative remark and ran his hand over our full-back's chest. It was not a good move. Josh reacted like the full-on army heterosexual he is and there was some pushing and shoving, but everything soon settled down. In fact, some of the players quite enjoyed the atmosphere of the place, and were seen going back the next night.

'Blah, blah, blah,' the guys said, repeating what had become our mantra at the end of the tour. 'Blah, blah, blah, let's go home.' We finally arrived at Heathrow, and rest became a reality.

Even when we were on holiday, I don't think any of us ever stopped thinking about the World Cup and what it could possibly represent in our careers and our lives. We were good enough to win it: we knew that. It was there for us, so every-one, individually, in his own way, had to make a decision to seize the opportunity. If we failed, it could not be for the want of trying.

So there was no lack of commitment when we gathered again for a training camp at the Pennyhill Park Hotel. We had huge confidence in each other and, importantly, we had confidence in Clive and his expert management team. What-ever they asked, we were going to do, without question. Pennyhill Park became our home from home. It was already a five-star establishment, but the hotel management had gone out of their way to create an ideal environment for rugby players. More than £15 million had been invested in a new spa and sports facility, each of our rooms had a four-poster bed and, specially for us, they had spent £150,000 on laying a perfect new rugby field for training. We heard they had done this in return for a guarantee from the RFU that the England team would use the hotel for five years. If so, it was a great deal for everyone.

Even when something went wrong, the people at Pennyhill Park stopped at nothing to put it right. For example, the ceiling of the new gym in the sports facility was built to stan-dard height but, unfortunately, this was not high enough for the taller members of our squad when they pushed weights above their heads. This was clearly a problem, but nobody – neither at Pennyhill Park nor within the England set-up – shrugged and said the players would have to make do. Instead, they created a new gym on a site beside our training field. A large marquee was placed on a strong concrete base, and rows of equipment and weights were installed. It was world-class, and a message was conveyed to everyone that in this campaign nothing would be left undone.

Clive and his experts had produced a weekly schedule, which meant that one week we would train every weekday and have the weekend off, and then the next week we would practise for only a couple of days. Every aspect of the programme had been calculated using scientific models for optimum physical performance. When I had started playing for England, the nature and length of training seemed to depend on the mood of the coach.

We were divided into groups, largely based on our position, but I was initially put in the Rehab Group. My back had been feeling sore and, although it was hopefully nothing more than the grumble of an injury that had flared and settled throughout my career, Clive said he didn't want me to take any chances.

Neil Back found himself in a similar position, and while the rest of the guys sweated through the mindless fitness stuff at the start of the camp the veteran loose forward and I stood apart and undertook a 'tailored' fitness programme. Our first task was to run twenty 100-metre sprints with thirty seconds' recovery in between. Neil was usually one of the fittest and fastest in the squad, and I was worried he would leave me behind and make me look slow. In fact, I kept ahead of him most of the time. Neil said his calf was hurting, but I was happy to take the praise for beating him.

Things were going quite well for me. No stomach pains, no headaches, no tiredness, and I was feeling pretty confident about my chances of getting into the final World Cup squad. There were four scrum-halves in the training group at Pennyhill Park and only three were going to make the trip, but the general consensus seemed to be that Matt, Gommers and I would get the nod, with Austin Healey being the unlucky one to miss out. I wasn't being complacent but, after finishing the summer tour as the first choice, I didn't see any reason to be anxious. First, I needed to get through the camp, which would be a challenge on its own.

A typical working day at Pennyhill Park began with an hour of vision training at six o'clock in the morning when Dave Alred, our specialist kicking coach, took us through sessions to improve awareness on the field. His voice soon began to sound like a rude awakening so early, and some ideas worked better than others. We played games with tennis balls and golf balls, sometimes with one eye covered by a patch, sometimes when we were only allowed to use one hand, and this was OK, but most of the guys battled to see the point when Dave attempted to disorientate us by playing loud music beside the field. I think you can sometimes try too hard to be innovative and different.

At seven o'clock, we moved to our gym in the marquee for seventy minutes of weight training, ranging from isolations to power weights to the strenuous one-handed pull-ups. This prepared us for a hearty breakfast and, since we were burning up so much energy, we were allowed to eat what we wanted. We had dedicated chefs, who knew each of us by name, and they quickly learned who liked what in their omelettes. Before long, we didn't have to order.

After a short break, we would assemble for a meeting where the coaching staff told us what to do and explained precisely what they hoped to gain from the day's training session. Every session would be clearly outlined, measured and assessed.

The actual rugby sessions were divided into sections, starting with hand–eye coordination exercises, where we usually enjoyed watching tight forwards like Julian White and Trevor Woodman dive around, trying to catch flying golf balls. We would then break into two groups, one focusing on defence and the other on attack, then vice versa. Last, the forwards would concentrate on their set pieces while the backs practised their moves and kicking. It was not unusual for us to be on our feet for around three hours, and everybody used to groan when Dave Alred asked for one more bit of concentration and effort.

There was sometimes some respite when we split up into our positional groups. Following my suggestion, Nigel Melville, a former England scrum-half, had been invited to join the camp and work with the No. 9s, and we had fun as a group, mostly hinging on the banter that crackled between Austin Healey and me. We were rivals, of course, and we tended to go at each other from dawn until night, bantering and bitching, taunting and teasing, winding each other up, calling each other names.

Austin produced at least four nicknames for me: he mocked my fast-receding hairline by calling me 'Les', after Les Cusworth, the almost bald former England fly-half, or 'Drawbridge' because it was all going up at the front. If it wasn't that, he called me 'silver spoon' because I'd gone to a private school, and 'Tim Nice But Dim' because he thought I had a middle-class accent.

He's got a decent sense of humour, and we all laughed, but I was ruthless in reply. Austin had been working incredibly hard to get his injured knee right, even to the point of spending five weeks with a specialist in the United States, and he was under pressure to perform and work his way back into contention. I admired the effort he was making to be part of the World Cup squad, spending so many hours in the gym, trying to get fit, but I wasn't going to let him get the better of me, so I gave him as much abuse as he gave me, and even made up a rhyme for him, which I repeated when he was getting the better of me.

> *I'm dead quick,*
> *I'm dead fast,*
> *But as a No. 9,*
> *I come last.*

We were motivating each other and, I'm sure, beneath all the insults there was a healthy degree of mutual respect. Austin might have been fighting a losing battle, because he had limited chances to prove himself after the injury, but he was brave.

Each day after training at Pennyhill Park, we were supposed to sleep for a couple of hours, but it wasn't just any nap. First, we had to sleep wearing special Lycra shorts, which hugged your legs and were supposed to squeeze the toxins out of your system. It has to be said they didn't look great on the forwards.

Then we were told to take more supplements to make us feel tired, so we would sleep better during the afternoon. Some of the guys said they felt like new patients at a mental asylum because, if we did exactly as we were told, each player would take twenty or thirty tablets and powdered drinks every day. So we behaved like older and wiser patients – and only took some of the pills.

Still, most of the players tried to get some sleep because they wanted to be prepared for the worst part of the day: a fitness session at the pitch. The backs were generally put through thirty-five minutes of gruelling speed-endurance work while the forwards focused on power but, to keep it interesting, the coaches sometimes organised competitions with mixed teams, combining running and cycling.

More often than not, the contest was won by the team that included Jonny Wilkinson. Our fly-half was extraordinarily fit, coming out on top in speed, power and general condition. A different player was named 'Trainer of the Week' every Friday but, if the truth were known, Jonny should have won it every week. In his commitment and in his pure ability, he was simply outstanding.

He, at least, had no reason to fear the hated testing sessions, which the coaches held at regular intervals, collecting data to show who was fit and who wasn't, who was trying and who was slacking. When I first started playing for England, the senior players used to skip these tests, usually blaming a timely hamstring strain that they 'didn't want to risk', but those days were long gone.

Our standard test used to be a timed three-kilometre run, seven and a half laps of mindless running. This was bearable for the half-backs and the back row, but the tight five and the speedsters tended to struggle. Now, at Pennyhill Park, we used the Omega system, where, early in the morning, they put pads on your chest and tracked your heart rate. These readings measured aerobic and anaerobic fitness and on one memorable occasion the coaches announced I had the best score. Everyone seemed impressed, and I puffed out my cheeks and tried to look cool. In fact, I was amazed. We had used the Omega system at Saracens and my very average readings then suggested they must have made some kind of mistake. Anyway, I certainly wasn't going to say anything and took the credit.

Another day I came top in the agility exercises, although the concept of me beating Jason Robinson in a directional-change test probably undermined the credibility of the system. In truth, so long as you weren't glaringly bad, you survived the tests.

Body fitness was followed by eye fitness. Clive brought in yet another enthusiastic specialist, who taught us to make better use of peripheral vision in match situations. Some of us looked a bit baffled at first, but we enjoyed the games with flashing numbers moving across a screen. Using 3-D goggles and other gadgets, our awareness began to improve. Each week brought a new gimmick, and at least it kept us all interested and alert.

Every day ended with a debriefing session, when each coach, in turn, reviewed the activities for which they had been responsible. This sometimes felt like a meeting for the sake of a meeting but, typically, the coach kept us on our toes by, every now and then, spicing up the meeting with a guest speaker. One of the best presentations was given by a guy who had walked unaided to the South Pole. He explained how much work he had put into his preparations, which Clive loved, but a group of ex-SAS security experts turned out to be the most entertaining speakers.

Soon after we arrived at Pennyhill, the coach told us he was going to hire people to infiltrate the camp and find out all our calls. A few of the players thought he was joking, and began to snigger. We knew the coach could be a maverick, but the idea of spying on your own players seemed ridiculous. Were these guys going to abseil into our rooms, or would they blindfold and interrogate us? Clive was deadly serious. 'Listen,' he snapped. 'Many of you know the Australians got hold of the Lions line-out calls in 2001 and how that affected the series. It has become a genuine issue, and we can't afford to get careless at the World Cup.'

His message went in one ear and out the other. As we became immersed in the camp, everybody forgot the coach's warning ... until the evening when the ex-SAS guys appeared at a team meeting and started to explain what they had been doing. They had sifted through rubbish bins at the hotel and learned our calls. They had watched us train from a hidden vantage point and knew our moves.

No names were mentioned, but the point was made crystal clear. Clive sat there, grinning from ear to ear because his plan had worked a treat and exposed our complacency. From that meeting onwards, the squad was instructed to take a series of precautions to protect our calls and other confidential information. A paper shredder was going to be installed in our team rooms at the World Cup and, after every meeting, we would have to either shred the handouts or keep them in a folder that would be stored, not in our rooms, but in a safe. When one guy suggested we should eat the secret documents, he was only half joking.

Second, we were told to watch out for bugs around the hotel. Photographs of the latest listening devices, concealed in everything from pens to mobile phones, were passed around and it was agreed that once we had arrived in Australia no team meeting would start until Tony Biscombe, our IT specialist, had cleared the room with his special bug-detecting device. This contraption was supposed to make a beeping noise when it detected something and, predictably, the guys amused themselves by sitting and mimicking the noise while Tony tried to work around them.

Third, we were taught to look out for a particular kind of van parked near our training venues. These vehicles could be fitted with video cameras to film our training sessions and particularly powerful microphones that would be able to record our voices from up to a hundred metres away and so record our calls.

Was Clive being paranoid? Most of us thought so, but we quite enjoyed the 007 stuff. The gadgets were fun and, at the back of our minds, we realised we had to be vigilant.

There was not much laid on in terms of entertainment, apart from a video games area, and most of us spent the evenings in our rooms. I was sharing with Alex King, the Wasps fly-half, who was struggling to recover from a knee injury, and we were usually too exhausted to do anything but watch TV or get an early night and recover for the next day.

An important element of our preparations was three warm-up internationals, against Wales in Cardiff followed by home and away matches against France. Clive's planning proved impeccable again because, as the tournament unfolded, these were the sides we met in the quarter-final and semi-final respectively.

England fielded a below-strength team to play Wales, but the understudies performed well and won comfortably. Andy Gomarsall looked sharp, and I sensed the competition for places in the World Cup squad was intensifying. After all our hard work at Pennyhill Park, we were approaching crunch time.

Austin Healey was chosen to play against France in Marseilles the next Saturday, in what was probably going to be his last opportunity to force his way into the World Cup squad. As the pressure on him mounted, so the banter between us increased. He called me posh; I told him he was standing on one leg in the last-chance saloon. He reminded me how he had been preferred to me for the 1997 Lions tour to South Africa, prompting me to point out who looked set to be in the World Cup squad and who didn't.

Nobody really enjoyed the trip to France. We moved from five-star Pennyhill Park to an underwhelming hotel in Marseilles, where the locks had to sleep with their feet resting on chairs at the end of the beds, and the facilities were not special. Everyone was complaining when we arrived, but we had a Test to play. The French had selected their strongest team, while we named another second-string side, which meant our long unbeaten run was under threat.

A fear of losing, the competition for places, the hotel: maybe all this combined to create the first signs of disharmony within the squad. The issue was the intensity of training in Marseilles: we were being pushed hard, which suited the guys outside the Test squad but upset those who were playing France on the Saturday.

Some of them refused to do any more running, and Dave Reddin, our fitness coach, complained about their attitude. I understood their point. Saturday was a huge match for them and they wanted to have fresh legs. A compromise was reached and they agreed to do a bit of low-key fitness work, but nothing more.

The game didn't go well, and we lost 16–17 to a French team who were going to be World Cup contenders in their own right, with a strong pack and classy backs. Austin tried his guts out, but he didn't have the stormer he needed, which meant Daws, Gommers and I felt more relaxed about our prospects. Sport is cruel at this level, but that's how it is and we all accept it.

We didn't have long to wait for revenge against the French. Clive declared he would pick his strongest team for the return international at Twickenham a week later, and I was really pleased to be named at No. 9, with Daws on the bench. Even Andy Robinson was talking up my selection, so

I was feeling confident, at ease with the world and was actually sleeping well at night.

Tempers flared again in training, and this time it was our turn, the guys playing at Twickenham, to complain about being 'beasted' just a few days before what was a major international. As we asked management to go easy on the physical training, some of those who had played in Marseilles chipped in and said it would be unfair unless we were treated the same as they had been. We eventually agreed to some light running, but most of us held back. A few hard looks were exchanged, but nobody bore any grudges.

The day before the match, I was training happily, barking at the forwards, popping out the passes, making breaks, when disaster struck. I will never understand why God gave me a glass back, but he did and I have had to suffer the consequences.

As I bent down to collect a ball, my back suddenly went into spasm and, in front of everybody, I collapsed in a heap. I realised I had to continue playing, so I stood up immediately and managed to get through till the end of the session, but I was getting a shooting pain in my back every time I bent forward. I was trying not to limp as I moved away from the field, desperately wanting to look OK, but my head was spinning. I didn't know what to do.

In normal circumstances, I would have withdrawn from the team on Saturday and rested, but this was not a normal time. I was the man in possession of the No. 9 jersey, and I could not give Daws a chance to play well and put me back on the bench. The physios took a look at me and asked how I was feeling.

'It's fine,' I lied. 'Nothing serious.'

They seemed to believe me but, inside, I felt devastated.

How could I play for England when I was hardly fit enough to bend over, let alone pass the ball? I went straight to my room, lay on the bed and telephoned Victoria to tell her what had happened. For once, on the eve of a major international, I didn't feel any anxiety at all about the game. This time, I was too busy worrying about my back.

After sleeping fitfully, I woke at around six in the morning and lay there, praying my back would not feel too bad. I sat up gingerly and stepped out of bed. It was still a bit sore, but it was bearable. I decided I would play and wouldn't give Daws another chance.

In the event, the French chose a second-string team, and we dominated from the kick-off. I started OK, but my back went after a quarter of an hour. It wasn't quite agony, but the coaches realised I was struggling and brought me off after thirty-eight minutes. So I sat on the bench and felt miserable as Daws buzzed at the heart of a big England win. That was it, I reckoned. Just when it mattered most, my dodgy back seemed to have cost me the opportunity of going to Australia as England's No. 1 scrum-half.

The announcement of the World Cup squad was imminent and everyone seemed nervous. Austin was still cracking jokes, saying he had two hopes of getting on the trip to Australia: 'Bob Hope and no hope'. I didn't say anything to him and he left me alone. After all the banter and ribbing, things were getting serious now.

Selection was made and, as we expected, Matt, Gommers and I were named as the three scrum-halves. After the disappointment of 1999, when injury kept me out of the tournament, after all the setbacks and after feeling so far out of England contention at the start of the year, I had made it. I was on the tour.

My roomie, Alex King, hadn't recovered from his knee injury and missed out. I tried to offer some words of friendly advice but, in that kind of situation, there is never any consolation. You have worked so hard, dedicated so much to something and, suddenly, it's all over. Alex took it well and said he'd bounce back.

Another friend, Mike Catt, was included in the World Cup squad, which pleased me. We had both been through so many ups and downs over the years, and we often joked about who had been dropped more times. I won that contest hands down. Before long, Mike and I were thrown together once again. He pulled his hamstring on our first day of training as the official World Cup squad and, not long afterwards, my back went in precisely the same place as it had before the France game. We were both placed on the injury list, where we worked hard to convince everyone that we would recover and be ready for the tour.

'You feeling OK?' I would ask Mike every morning.

'Yeah, I'm fine,' he would reply blankly. 'You?'

'Good,' I would say.

We continued this charade, each knowing we were both much more concerned about our physical condition than we were ready to admit to each other, let alone the management. At one stage, Clive made a point of warning Catty that he had better be fit, and that prompted my friend to speak openly to me.

'I'm struggling now,' he said, 'but as long as I can get on board that flight to Australia, there's not much they can do and I am sure I'll be right in time for the tournament.'

I took the same view. 'Get on the plane and hope for the best' was my attitude. Some people might say we might have been letting the team down by not being completely honest about our injuries, but there are times in your career when you have to be selfish. I was not going to miss yet another World Cup because of my back. Whatever anyone says, anybody in our place would have done the same. So Catty and I kept up our act that we felt sure we would be right and, with a bit of luck and a lot of determination, both got through the period before the squad left for Australia.

It was an exciting time. After spending a few last days at home, we gathered at a hotel to receive our kit. The players all knew Clive had claimed the responsibility for selecting our formal wear at the World Cup, which was a worry because, in the past, he had got us wearing tweed jackets, purple cords and brown shoes. So it was with considerable relief that we tried on our surprisingly decent light grey suits, even if they did have to be worn with the same, now in-famous, brown shoes.

Our official kit sponsors, Nike, were generous, providing the players with vast quantities of training kit, although this made the task of packing even more difficult. Over the years, I had learned to travel light on international tours, which meant taking as few of my own clothes, but this time the matter was not quite so simple.

First, there was a commercial balance to be found. We were supposed to wear Nike clothes all the time because they were the official England suppliers, but most of the players also had their own contracts with personal kit sponsors. I was associated with Reebok, and I packed as much of their gear as I dared.

Then, there was the question of quantity. On normal England tours, most players packed a minimum amount of kit and discarded it as we went along, but the World Cup trip was different. If we did win the trophy in Australia, everyone would want to have kept as much kit as possible, to get it signed by the players and eventually sold at a benefit auction or for charity. With this in mind, most people seemed to be packing more gear than usual, just in case every garment turned out to be a collector's item.

In the days before our departure, the level of expectation in the country was clear. You could sense it in the players' body language, you could feel it in the way Clive operated and you could even see it in the eyes of complete strangers who walked up and wished you luck in Australia: this England team was not aiming to compete, do our best and see what happens. We aimed to win.

The squad was inundated with literally thousands of goodwill messages before we left London, from the good and the great, but two video messages particularly amused us.

The first film was sent from the Everton football team to one of their most dedicated supporters, Matt Dawson. It began with the manager, David Moyes, offering some words of encouragement, but it was Wayne Rooney who stole the show. The seventeen-year-old prodigy showed us how to tackle by running thirty metres and clattering into a team-mate who was holding a pad. With his team-mates all laughing, Wayne got up with a huge smile on his face and said in his strong Scouse accent: 'Go on, Matt, beat those Aussies!'

We also watched a video where our team was likened to the cast of *The Lord of the Rings*, the Oscar-winning film. Most of the forwards were 'orcs' while the starring parts were given to the big names and the backs, and Clive was Gandalf. It was brilliantly done, and the players loved it because we had visited the set and cast of the film while touring New Zealand earlier in the year.

The message wasn't lost on us either. Just as the film based itself on a great mission to achieve something, to find the ring, so our trip was focused on one goal: winning the World Cup. Some of these motivational, inspirational exercises work and others don't, but the England 2003 *Lord of the Rings* video hit the spot.

In previous years, departing England rugby squads had grown used to being showered with gifts. I recalled the days before we left for the 1995 World Cup in South Africa, when we were given leather jackets, stacks of clothes, extra gifts for the wives and girlfriends, and many, many crates of Laurent-Perrier champagne.

Those were the joys of the amateur era. Now, as highly paid professional players, we were each given just one present when we boarded the bus to take us from the hotel to Heathrow airport. We received a pair of cufflinks, one of which contained a fragment of the actual England flag that had been flown on the roof of the stand at Twickenham, and the other enclosed personal messages from our families. The guys quietly read these notes as the bus picked its way through the London traffic.

It was a neat touch, as carefully conceived and impeccably implemented as every aspect of our preparations. From the months spent at Pennyhill Park, through all the training sessions and team briefings, through the three warm-up internationals, through the naming of the squad, we had slowly come together. As I sat on the bus, I wriggled in my seat. Even my back was not feeling too bad. No question, we were ready.

The razzmatazz began when we arrived at Heathrow airport. Jonny Wilkinson found himself surrounded by screaming fans as soon as he stepped off the bus and, with Martin Johnson, was whisked to a VIP entrance and on to the Executive Lounge. The rest of us were left to deal with the genuine fans who had come to see us off, and the dreaded professional autograph hunters.

We had learned to recognise most of these people because they were always to be seen hanging around our hotel and waiting for us at airports, and we despised them because they posed as genuine fans collecting our autographs when, in reality, they were running a scam to get signed items sold over the Internet. This little activity had become big business, so we developed our own counter-strategy. We didn't want to turn anyone down and appear rude, but when any of us was requested to sign something, we all decided to ask: 'Who shall I make this out to?'

They would then have to say a name. This was no problem for a real fan, who was delighted to get a personalised autograph, but it didn't help the businessmen because an England jersey signed 'Best wishes to John' was not as easy to sell as one that featured only the signatures of the England players.

As we were congratulating ourselves on effectively closing the industry, some of the guys started to notice we were being asked to sign a remarkable number of jerseys and other items for people by the name of 'Ali'. It didn't take us long to realise the conmen were joining up the dot on the 'i' of 'Ali' to make an 'l', and marketing the items with a generic 'Best wishes to All'. From that day, we have generally refused to sign any items for individuals called 'Ali', which is probably a little bit harsh on true fans who happen to have that name, but we all feel strongly about this issue, and we won't let them win.

So we signed a few autographs at Heathrow, for anyone

not called 'Ali', and eventually made our way through Passport Control and on to the British Airways Executive Lounge. As usual, everything had been arranged to make our lives as easy as possible. We had effectively checked in for the flight at our hotel reception in central London, receiving our boarding passes and handing in luggage that we would next see in our hotel rooms in Perth.

'Give us superstar performances, and you will be treated like superstars,' Clive Woodward always liked to say, and he certainly kept his side of the deal. He knew the players hated waiting around airports, so he ensured that did not happen. He knew the players enjoyed extra space on the aircraft, so he insisted the England team always travelled in either First or Business Class.

Clive relentlessly put the players first, but he had excelled himself during the 2001 tour to North America, when he saw we would have to make a couple of flight connections to travel from one side of the United States to the other. He told the RFU this was unacceptable, and insisted they spend another £50,000 hiring a private jet to take us directly from one venue to the next. We flew like millionaires, in plush leather seats, being served endless food.

The Union probably sighed every time the coach put forward another request, but the players appreciated his approach and we understood that, so long as we kept winning, the RFU officials would continue to give Clive whatever he wanted.

Faced by the prospect of spending almost two hours in the BA Executive Lounge at Heathrow, we did what rugby players usually do with time to spare and started feeding. A quick raid to Burger King was out of the question because our nutritional experts/police were around, so we contented ourselves by pigging out on every snack, sandwich, biscuit and blueberry muffin in the lounge.

The gluttony ceased when we were ushered off to pose for a promotional photograph with some of BA's best-looking air hostesses on the steps leading up to the plane. Nobody complained about mixing with the girls while hundreds of photographers snapped their cameras at us. I had seen similar pictures featuring the England football squad on their way to compete at a major tournament, but it struck me we were different: we were uglier, we were paid a lot less and we stood a decent chance of winning.

Once aboard, the guys wasted no time in changing out of our grey suits into something more comfortable. It would probably have been more polite if we had formed an orderly queue and changed one after the other in the toilet, but nobody could be bothered and we casually started undressing in the cabin. Some of the air hostesses discreetly looked away while these strapping, muscular players stripped down to their underwear, hid one another's shorts and messed about, but the others seemed to enjoy the view. The players were all laughing and joking, playing around with seats that collapsed into beds, getting to grips with the gadgets. Everyone was upbeat and excited.

Experience had taught me it is important to be sitting next to a mate on these long thirty-six-hour trips to Australia, and I was fortunate to find myself allocated the seat beside Jason Leonard, not only the most capped prop forward in the history of the game but also one of the funniest, most down-to-earth guys in the squad.

It didn't take us long to start wallowing in nostalgia, recalling stories from the good old days, and we chuckled as Jase reminded me what had happened when we headed for the airport on our way to the 1995 World Cup in South Africa, and Graham Dawe got left behind at the hotel. He arrived in the foyer just as we were pulling out of the drive, panicked and sprinted after the team bus through the streets of Richmond. Some of the press photographers were still hanging around, and they got some great shots.

The pilot came on the public address system and welcomed the England rugby team on his flight. He then wished us luck at the World Cup, prompting a wave of applause to flood through the 747 jumbo jet. It sounded strange and unusual, but we appreciated the support of our fellow passengers at 30,000 feet.

Management kept working. Our team doctor walked down the aisle, offering us sleeping pills, Vitamin C tablets and another drug to prevent deep-vein thrombosis, which had been all over the media and affects passengers on long-haul flights. He also told us to reduce the threat of DVT by walking up and down as often as possible and putting on tight knee-length surgical stockings, which everyone said, like the Lycra shorts, looked lovely on the forwards.

Everybody was having a good time but, beneath the smile, I was starting to worry. My back was beginning to ache again, and it seemed unlikely that I would be able to train when we arrived in Australia. I was concerned about what the coaches would say and decided to tell Jase how I was feeling.

'Listen, mate,' he replied, speaking with the benefit of more experience than anyone else in the side. 'Get out there and see how it goes, or they will have you on a flight home before you can say "boo".'

The flight started to drag, and I couldn't resist the temptation to stand up every twenty minutes or so and test my back. Pretending to stretch, I would bend forward and, every time, severe pain would shoot through my back. Bloody hell, I thought. I watched a film and then started to worry about sleeping. I didn't want to take the pills, but then I didn't want to stay awake either.

Jase didn't have a problem. He asked for a glass of red wine and was soon snoring happily. Nobody else in the squad would have dared to drink alcohol in front of the management, but Jase wasn't a schoolkid and he didn't need anyone to tell him how to relax. I began watching another film, but finally relented, took a single tablet and was eventually lulled to sleep by the slow, steady rhythm of Jase's snoring as it vibrated through my seat.

Our trip to Australia included a stopover in Singapore, and we blearily trooped into the transit terminal, ready and willing to wave our credit cards at the duty-free shops. Most of us pored over the portable DVD players and iPods, and even managed to devise a contest to see who could negotiate the best bargain. We usually managed to create a competition out of anything.

A few of the guys were trying out some incredible automatic massage chairs, which gave an awesome head-to-toe experience. I wandered over and was tempted to spend my bonus on one of the chairs, but the hassle of shipping the thing back to Hertfordshire put me off and I kept my credit card in my wallet.

The second leg of the trip flew by, and we weren't feeling too bad when we eventually arrived in Perth. There were some journalists, a couple of TV crews and a few diehard supporters waiting to meet us at the airport, but they immediately clamoured around Jonny and Johnno, and pretty much left the rest of us alone.

Our sport is the third most popular form of rugby in Australia, after League and Australian Rules, and it was almost nonexistent in Western Australia, so most bystanders at Perth airport seemed to have no idea who we were. They tended to stand, staring, trying to work out why we were all wearing the kit.

Most of us were familiar with the hotel, after our visit at the end of the summer tour, and we were pleased to find we all had our own single rooms. Apparently, the tournament organisers had provided players with twin rooms, sharing, but Clive had gone ahead and booked singles and persuaded the RFU to pay the difference. Nobody would ever claim we weren't being given the opportunity to succeed and, for that, the Union suits deserve plenty of credit.

The players slipped easily into a routine of gym, physio, training and spending time in our private games room at the hotel, where I managed to stay unbeaten on the table tennis table. Some others, including Catty, Daws and Iain Balshaw, played backgammon, often with small bets on the side. In years gone by, England tour squads operated sharp card schools, often with thousands of pounds on the table, but they had gone now. With a bit of darts and chess thrown in, we managed to keep ourselves amused.

Our other main activity was eating. It isn't surprising that players often put on weight during overseas tours because there is always plenty of food in the team room, and it is easy to sit there devouring all kinds of sandwiches and biscuits.

I slept well for the first two nights in Perth but on the third night the jet lag suddenly kicked in and I couldn't get to sleep. I lay awake for hours and, at five o'clock in the morning, was wandering down to the team room, not knowing what to do except stuff my face with food. I had already taken two pills and had promised not to wake the team doctor in the middle of the night.

Quarter to six in the morning in Perth was quarter to eight the previous evening at home, so I phoned Victoria, and my wife calmly told me to take a hot bath and not worry so much. Training was scheduled to start at ten o'clock, and I was growing concerned about feeling completely knackered. I didn't even dare think my old sleeping problems might possibly have returned.

Eventually, I went down to breakfast and was relieved to hear that Dan Luger and others were also suffering from jet lag. They hadn't slept either and it seemed they'd spent most of the night playing darts in the team room. I must have just missed them. Hearing them talk about their problems made me feel a lot better, though. Maybe it was jet lag, after all. Perhaps I was OK. After a week, we all settled into Australian time and were sleeping better.

Afternoons were spent on the local coffee shop circuit, and I generally found myself going out in a group with Stuart Abbott and Mark Regan. We used to get at each other about being tight, and I teased Mark because he was always asking what the win bonus was for each match. So every time we went out we played a game of spoof to decide who would pick up the bill.

In spoof, every player takes anything between none and three coins in their closed hand, and each of us in turn has to guess the total number of coins in our hands. It requires intelligent guessing and, when Mark was the first to lose, Stuart and I made sure to order the largest cup of coffee and the biggest slice of chocolate cake in the shop. The bill came to the equivalent of more than £25, and Mark paid.

He lost again the next day, and the day after that. Mark said he wanted to stop the game because it was getting out of hand, but we kept playing and, when I lost, he rammed it back in my face by ordering a main course from the menu and offering pieces of cake to anybody who walked past. With such ongoing antics, we passed slow days, waiting for the tournament to start.

The 2003 Rugby World Cup was finally launched, in Perth at least, with a cocktail party for the five national squads based in the city. We arrived to find our group rivals sitting in separate areas of the hilltop venue, watching each other cautiously. The mood quickly improved, the teams began to interact and I caught up with my old rival, Springbok No. 9 Joost van der Westhuizen.

Stuart Abbott knew many of the South African players, having spent most of his formative years in that country, but when he started talking Afrikaans, Mark Regan and I decided to wind him up by calling him a traitor. It became quite funny: we meant he was a traitor because he was talking our opposition's language, while the South Africans reckoned he was a traitor because he had decided to play international rugby for England. Everybody was smiling except for Stuart, who didn't particularly enjoy the joke.

The Western Samoans were typically relaxed, chatting easily to everyone, but most of the players from Georgia and Uruguay just stood there, in awe of their rugby heroes. Several of them asked if they could have photographs taken with Jonny, and he was happy to oblige. The atmosphere was turning strange, so we were given our caps, had a full squad photograph taken and hurried back to the sanctuary of our hotel as soon as possible.

I was managing to get through the training sessions, but

my back was far from 100 per cent and I was quite relieved when Daws was named in the team to play our opening match of the tournament, against Georgia. In normal circumstances, I would have been upset to be back on the bench but, since I still couldn't bend without pain, I was happy to be named among the substitutes.

In fact, we had all known the Test XV some days before, when the management announced a team for training. As usual, they told us: 'Please don't read anything into this, but the following players should please put on a bib.' And the players all smirked, because it was obviously the starting team in all but name. Many of us couldn't see the point of acting out the pointless charade.

Our preparation to play Georgia was limited due to the fact that we didn't know any more about them than what we could see from a bad-quality videotape of their qualifying victory over Russia. They were obviously a fiery lot, but they didn't look remotely prepared for the physical onslaught of the England pack.

If they were worried, so was I. My back went again at training on the day before the game. Clive walked straight over to me and asked how I was feeling. I said I was fine, of course.

'It's happening too often,' he said. 'KB, this is the World Cup and you had better make sure you are right.'

'It's no problem,' I lied again. 'I'll be fine.'

The stakes were getting higher and I was becoming increasingly concerned, but I got a decent night's sleep and, amazingly, felt fine when I woke up on the morning of the game. I developed a plan to get through the rest of the day: no bending to test the back, warm up carefully and only then start practising my passing.

We arrived at the stadium and found the England changing room had been decked out in St George's flags. Inspirational signs had been stuck on the wall. One read: 'We are England, and we are here for one thing, to win.' Someone turned up the volume of the music, and the guys started to get psyched.

As I sat alone in my corner of the dressing room, it seemed my strategy was going well. I had warmed up and my back felt fine. Then, just as I was strapping my left ankle, a sudden, sharp pain shot through my lower back. It had gone again. I stood and tested it by bending forward. This time it was bad, really bad.

Bollocks, I thought to myself. I'll say nothing and get through the day. If I pull out now, that'll be the end of my tournament and they'll put me on the next flight to London. I tried to stretch, tried to warm the muscles, but it wasn't getting any better. My last hope was to take some painkillers, so I went through to the doctor and asked him for a Voltarol injection in my arse cheek.

Please work, please work. My mind was racing. I could hardly believe I had come so far, and worked so hard, to find myself in this terrible situation. I sat in my place for another five minutes. It was no good. The pain was the same. If I was summoned off the bench, I would have been useless. I couldn't even bend over, let alone play for England in the World Cup. I faced the reality and limped away to find the coach in the changing room next door.

'Clive, you're not going to believe this,' I said, 'but my back has gone. I can't play. I'm going to have to withdraw.'

His response was brilliant. He told me I had made exactly the right call and said I had been brave to withdraw in the interests of the team. 'But, KB,' he added, 'I am worried about you, and we're going to fly in a replacement in case you don't recover. That's just a precaution, but we need some improvement.'

I had a word with Johnno as well, and the captain was great, telling me not to worry and to focus on getting fit for the rest of the tournament, but I felt dejected and disconsolate as I plodded back to the other changing room. My place on tour was in real jeopardy, and my arse was feeling sore from the injection.

Finding my mobile in my kitbag, I quickly phoned Victoria and then my parents to tell them what had happened, so they wouldn't be surprised when they were watching on TV and I didn't appear among the substitutes. They all sounded even more disappointed than me, but there was nothing anybody could do.

Andy Gomarsall took my place on the bench. Fortunately, he had brought his kit with him to the stadium and, after my mishap, it became a firm rule that all the driftwood (a collective noun used for members of the squad who were neither in the starting side nor on the bench) had to take their kit to every match, just in case they were summoned into the squad at the last moment.

So I watched from the stands as our campaign began. Clive had told us to get the basics right and make certain we didn't show the South Africans any of our moves ahead of the important match against them a week later. He also warned us not to be complacent, and our attitude was reflected in Johnno's decision to kick for goal, rather than run, when we won our first penalty. We proceeded to dominate the match in the rain and won 84–6 without ever getting into our rhythm or looking like potential champions.

My decision to withdraw turned out to have been the right call when Daws came off with a sore calf muscle. If I had pretended to be OK, I would have had to play with a dodgy back. It could easily have been humiliating but, when we returned to the hotel after the victory, Clive made a point of saying he was pleased I had put the team first and everybody should do the same if they ever found themselves in that situation. I kept quiet, knowing that if the match had been my last chance, I would probably have taken the gamble.

So while everyone else looked forward to the biggest match of the group phase, England against South Africa in Perth, analysing the two teams and dissecting the form, I found myself locked away in my own private struggle to get fit. My situation was clear: either I made a swift recovery or I would be sent home.

As he had said, Clive was arranging for another scrum-half to fly from England to Australia as cover for me. It should have been Austin Healey, but my friend's luck wasn't improving: after missing out on the England squad, he had gone back to his club, Leicester, and pulled out of the next match with an injury. So when they needed a potential replacement for me, he couldn't be considered and they called on Martyn Wood, from Bath.

It wasn't easy for Woody, because he arrived in Perth but was not permitted to join the squad until a final decision had been made on me. That meant he had to stay at a separate hotel, and we were only allowed to meet him outside, at a coffee shop or somewhere. I could see he was excited, which was natural, but he was decent to me as well. It was a tough situation for everybody.

I had to get fit again. The prospect of flying home on my own almost before the World Cup had got under way was too terrible to contemplate and, early in that week before the South Africa match, I went for a few long walks, alone, running over everything in my mind, preparing myself to recover and get strong.

Each time I returned to our hotel after these bouts of soulful introspection, I saw Jonny practising his passing and his kicking, on his own, in the park across the road. I remember thinking to myself, if only I had put in the same hours of practice as him and worked harder in the gym, building up the strength of my back, I probably wouldn't be in this mess.

I spoke to Victoria on the telephone for almost an hour every night, and she kept me positive and optimistic, telling me to hang in there and try everything. I had another chat with the team doctor and asked whether it might be possible to do something last-minute to get me right for Saturday. He called a surgeon, who suggested I could try some 'facet' injections under an X-ray.

'It involves putting steroids into the facets and discs,' the surgeon told me on the phone. 'There's no guarantee it will work, and it may make it worse, but you've got nothing to lose.'

He was right, so I agreed to have the procedure and went off to a hospital early the next morning. The team doctor came with me, which I appreciated, and they gave me seven injections in all, each as painful as the other, and I had to bite on a towel to stop myself screaming out loud as the needles plunged. Come on, I said to myself, a little pain now could put me right.

After the procedure, the doctor told me to sign a form, which outlined exactly which steroids had been injected. I was under the impression that this would protect me if anything showed up in any future drugs test, after the game or something, but I wasn't sure and I didn't ask in case I got the wrong answer. I was trying to get fit, trying to stay on tour. That was my only concern.

'KB, you feeling OK?' Clive asked, back at the hotel.

'Yeah, fine,' I replied, telling the truth for once.

An hour or so after the injections, my back was feeling great. I talked to the team doctor again and we agreed I would rest until the next day, Thursday, when the three injured players – Daws, Richard Hill and I – would have formal fitness tests. It was not an ideal situation for Clive, or anyone, having the top two scrum-halves in doubt forty-eight hours before a huge match, but the coach seemed calm and I prepared for the do-or-die examination.

That's exactly what it was for me, but not for Hilly. The loose forward had not been given the same ultimatum – to get fit or be sent home – and I enjoyed ribbing him about being Clive's blue-eyed boy and getting special treatment. In truth, I knew my team-mate for Saracens and England was just too good to lose.

So when Daws and I arrived at the training ground on that fateful Thursday morning, three outcomes were still possible. If I failed the fitness test, I would be sent home. If I passed and Daws passed, I would be on the bench for Saturday. If I passed and Daws failed, I would start the game against South Africa.

One of our physios, Barney Kenney, came over to take me through the test, while another went off with Daws. The pressure was on and, as we started with a gentle ten-minute jog, I noticed Clive arrive and take a seat on the clubhouse balcony overlooking the field. I wondered what was going through his mind. After all his meticulous planning, he might have been almost as nervous as me. After the running, we did some changes in direction, and that went OK. Barney asked me to do some passing. It was going to be the first time I had bent forward in four days ... I passed once, and felt fine; again, no problem; again, no pain at all.

Adrenaline, euphoria, relief and excitement, whatever: it was all gushing through my system. The injections had worked, and I was flying. Swerve, pass, sidestep, kicking: I felt no discomfort at all and an expression of sheer glee spread across my face. I glanced up at Clive and he gave me the thumbs-up.

I had passed, and was staying on tour, and I quickly glanced across at Daws to see how he was getting along. He appeared to be going well, so I headed off for a shower, content to be safely on the bench against South Africa. Five minutes later, Daws came into the changing room, looking absolutely gutted.

'Well done, mate,' he said. 'You're playing on Saturday.'

My instant reaction to the news that he had failed his fitness test, and that I would be starting the big game on Saturday, was the usual blend of excitement and alarm. Of course I was thrilled to be playing for England in the World Cup but, given everything that had happened with my back, I had reconciled myself to the prospect of sitting on the bench and maybe coming on for a tester for the last ten minutes. Unfortunately, life is not so predictable; or rather, my life never seems to be that predictable.

Play it again, Clive. For the umpteenth time in my career, I had been pushed to the brink of total rejection, only to find myself suddenly back in the England No. 9 jersey, with forty-eight hours to prepare for what seemed the biggest match of my career. I was starting to feel like a cat with nine lives, although I had forgotten quite how many of those lives I had used. Did I have any left? Could I rise to the occasion again? A few weeks short of my thirty-second birthday, did I still have it in me to play at this level? All I knew for sure was that being a 'Comeback Kid' wasn't getting any easier.

My recovery meant Martyn Wood was no longer required, but he took the wasted trip around the world in good heart, and caught the next flight back to London. Sport is like that. The lines are so fine. He had been just a click of my unpredictable back away from playing in the World Cup, but instead he was going home.

The positive spin on all this drama was that I hadn't had any time to worry about playing South Africa, or feel the pressure of a game that we needed to win to finish top of our group and so, in all probability, all other things being equal, avoid playing the All Blacks and Australia on our possible path to the final. I was more focused on my back and trying not to do anything stupid.

I had a scare during a team run on the Friday morning when, halfway through, I thought my back had popped again but, after a moment of blind panic, it seemed to settle. Something had clicked, but it wasn't that bad. We ran through some moves afterwards and, at the back of every ruck and maul, I called for the forwards to 'pop' the ball up into my hands because I didn't have the confidence to bend right down and take the ball from the ground. I knew I had to take care, so I was trying to nurse my back along.

I hadn't said anything to anyone and, when the forwards and backs divided to practise separately, I tried to avoid having to bend over and collect the ball from the ground by flicking it up with the end of my boot, like a footballer, and then passing. I thought I'd got away with it, until I saw Clive walking towards me.

'KB, you don't look great,' he said. 'Are you OK?'

'Of course.' I smiled.

Nothing more was said, and I got through the session. There was no problem, I told myself, no problem, but I rested for most of the day and, to my amazement, got a good eight hours' sleep that night. I woke up on the Saturday morning and felt absolutely fine, and, almost for the first time, began to concentrate on South Africa and another duel with Joost van der Westhuizen.

Our game plan was straightforward: be very, very physical all over the field and dominate the set pieces. Clive also wanted us to target the Springbok half-backs. They had selected Louis Koen to play fly-half, and some of the guys thought he looked slow to get his kicks away. We had practised charging down kicks regularly during our preparations, and Phil Larder, our defensive coach, was obviously getting excited about the prospect of one of us catching the South African No. 10 trying to clear his lines.

We also focused on Joost because he was such a key player for them and we felt that if we could disrupt him, we would be able to upset their entire team. He had looked sharp in their first match, scoring three tries against Uruguay, but we planned to wind him up by holding him down for a few extra seconds at ruck time and also to put pressure on his pass. I was pleased when Phil told me I had complete freedom to go for Joost at the base of the scrum, rather than just fold into our defensive line as usual.

There was an incredible atmosphere at the Subiaco Oval. There may not have been much of a rugby tradition in the city, but the organisers had worked hard to generate public interest in the tournament and, supplemented by thousands of expatriate South Africans in Perth and our substantial travelling support, the crowd were really buzzing when we started our warm-up.

Determined to take no risks with my back, I planned to warm up with a gentle jog before I tried to bend down and, remembering what had happened before the Georgia game, I even made certain I was warm before I began to strap up my ankles. When I had asked the doc for another Voltarol injection, and a suppository, just to be on the safe side, I finally felt I was ready.

Johnno was screaming at us.

'******* physicality!' our captain yelled, psyching us all into match mode. '******* physicality! That's what I want!'

After all the build-up, the game started slowly for both sides, as though we were testing each other out, but my back was feeling 100 per cent perfect and I soon got into my passing game, always pushing forward, shouting at the pack, looking for gaps.

We played a move on the right, then switched to attack down the left. Reaching the red zone, deep inside their half, I recalled Clive saying we had to get points on the board as early as possible, so I made our prearranged signal to try a drop goal. Jonny slipped back into the pocket and everything was set. I got the ball from the maul and threw the pass ... only to find Neil Back steaming round, in the way. He managed to catch my pass and tried a drop goal of his own, which dribbled pitifully along the ground.

It was a mess. I shouted at Backy for mucking up the move, and he blamed me for passing to him. The game was unfolding as a dogfight, and we were making mistakes. At one stage, when Koen missed a kick at goal, Will Greenwood inexplicably forgot to dot the ball down behind our line, so when he passed the ball forward for the 22 drop-out, the referee had to blow for a forward pass and gave South Africa a scrum on our line.

Everyone was wondering what the hell was going on, and this was dangerous because Joost had scored so many tries from exactly this kind of position. I steeled myself to mark him and, just as the No. 8 tried to feed him the ball, I managed to tag his arm and make him nudge the ball forward.

The referee spotted the knock-on, and promptly awarded us a scrum. As I prepared to put the ball in, I muttered a quiet word of thanks to Dewi Morris, my rival for the No. 9 jersey in the early years with England and a recognised expert in this particular ploy. As soon as he retired, I telephoned him and begged him to pass on the trade secret. Dewi was obliging, and I have been successfully hounding No. 8s ever since.

The Springboks wasted a few other chances and at half time the game was still in the balance. Johnno pulled us together in the changing room and got stuck in. 'Sort out the line-outs,' he said. 'Put more pressure on the kicks and start building the score. Come on, we can't throw this away now.' Lawrence Dallaglio also said his piece, urging us to produce a massive half.

Neatly, the match did turn on a charge-down. To Phil Larder's undisguised delight, Lewis Moody closed in on Koen, got the crucial touch and Will Greenwood followed through to score a try. We had edged ahead, and Jonny's goal-kicking kept us there. Without ever playing to our potential, we secured a 25–6 victory from what was a typically bruising physical contest with the Boks.

I played the full match, my back had come through without any problem and I felt reasonably pleased. It seemed to me that I had man-marked Joost quite effectively, cleared a lot of ball, made my tackles and generally bossed the game.

At least Johnno must have thought I did OK, because he gave me a huge bear hug and said 'well done' when the two of us were summoned to appear for the media at the post-match press conference.

Most of the journalists congratulated me on my display, and I got some very positive coverage the next day in all the newspapers – except one. For some reason, the main rugby correspondent of the *Sunday Times*, Stephen Jones, has never rated me. So, while I was getting marks like eight or nine out of ten in most of the papers, I got only a mediocre five out of ten in his column.

Andy Robinson didn't seem too impressed either. He said the forwards hadn't played well in the contact area, and he reckoned I was to blame. I waited for the assistant coach to mention anything positive about my performance, and waited in vain. Well, I thought, if Robbo gets his way, I'll be right back on the bench.

Clive seemed pleased with my efforts the following day, but he was far more animated about Lawrence Dallaglio, who had been cited by the South Africans for punching Thinus Delport. It seemed pretty innocuous but, taking no chances, the management called Richard Smith, the tour party's own Queen's Counsel, to ensure the case went nowhere. It appeared the issue had been complicated by Lol's off-the-cuff remark after the game that he had only given Delport 'a little slap'. The coach was furious and told us all to keep our mouths shut.

We left Perth that afternoon and flew to Melbourne where we would play our next group match, against Western Samoa, in the same Colonial Stadium where we had beaten the Wallabies four months before. Familiarity bred confidence, but most of us were intrigued to see what team Clive was going to select. Some of the bigger names would have liked a rest, but we all knew the hard-running, physical Western Samoans could never be taken lightly.

The coach erred on the side of caution and chose a strong side but, in so doing, he annoyed some of the people who had still not played a match in the tournament. A few of them wondered aloud why they had been brought all the way to Australia if they weren't going to get a game, but Clive was always going to do only what he believed was necessary to win. Daws had recovered, and was well enough to start, and Gommers sat on the bench.

It didn't take long for Clive's decision to be vindicated, because the Samoans had done their homework. They attacked us out wide, where other teams, especially the French, had shown our defensive system could be broken. In recent years, England sides had tended to deploy an up-and-out defence, or a slide defence, as it was often known. This ensured nobody ever got through down the middle, but it did leave some space around the edges.

We were being exposed and it wasn't a massive surprise when they fielded one of our kicks deep in their own half, spread the ball wide, advanced down the flank and, after a couple of impressive shimmies, scored a try through Semo Sititi, their captain who played for the Borders regional team in Scotland.

Samoa led 16–13 at half time, but we improved in the second half, using our stronger pack to deny them possession and squeeze them out of the game. We had been given a fright, and yet again had performed well below par, but the 35–22 win kept us on course to qualify for the quarter-finals as group winners. Or so we thought, until another controversy began to engulf us.

In the course of making a substitution, we had played around thirty seconds of the match against Western Samoa with sixteen players on the field. We had technically broken the law, and several Australian journalists began to speculate we could even be docked points for the infringement. That was a joke, but we were playing in a World Cup on foreign soil and could take nothing for granted. Once again, the management called in a Queen's Counsel.

Ironically, before the game, Clive had told us he wasn't happy with the speed our substitutes were getting on to the field, and he instructed us to sprint on as quickly as possible, ignoring the official on the touchline if necessary. 'I never want to defend with fourteen men,' he said, 'so, subs, get on as quickly as possible.'

That's exactly what we did. Dan Luger was called from the substitutes' bench during the second half and, as one of fastest in our squad, he ran straight out and joined the game, before the official had sanctioned the substitution and before Mike Tindall had had time to get off the field. So we briefly played with sixteen men, and this upset the fifth official on the touchline, a New Zealander called Steve Walsh, who was probably feeling ignored. Dave Reddin, our fitness coach, had been trying to organise the substitution from his designated position by the side of the field but he found himself caught between Clive, who was sitting high in the stands, telling him over the radio link to get Dan on as quickly as possible, and the touchline official who was instructing him to wait.

Tempers started to fray and Walsh made some derogatory remarks about the England team to Dave. This didn't go down well. More words were exchanged, someone squirted water from a plastic bottle and there was an incident in the tunnel after the game. Dave said Walsh tripped him, but the official said he had been assaulted and made a complaint to the match commissioner.

So the QC had two issues to deal with: our mistake of playing with sixteen men on the field, and the assault charge against Dave. Clive called a team meeting, and some of the guys laughed as the coach outlined exactly what had happened. 'Listen, this isn't funny,' Clive barked. 'We could get into serious trouble here.'

The QC asked if any players had heard or seen anything, and Dan Luger was able to confirm Dave's version of what was said on the touchline. A couple of others had seen the incident in the tunnel, and said the allegation of assault was rubbish. The QC took everything into account and said Dan needed to fly to Sydney for the hearing, which was a pain for him, especially when it turned out he didn't have much to do when he got there.

In any case, we got a decent result. We were fined £10,000 for having sixteen players on the field, which Clive cheekily said should be passed on to the Samoans because they had refused to make a fuss about the incident. The New Zealand official was suspended for one game, and Dave was banned from the touchline for our next couple of matches, though he was cleared of the assault charges. It could have been far worse.

Needless to say, we gave him a bit of stick for the next week or so, humming the soundtrack from *Rocky* whenever he was around, but we missed him beside the field. Dave was close to the players. Of a similar age to us and passionate for us to win, he felt bad about the whole saga but, from our point of view, he had stood up for the team, and there was nothing wrong in that.

Three wins in three matches gave us a strong position on top of the group and, with just Uruguay to come, the mood in the squad became more relaxed. It was almost as though we had cleared the first hurdle and could now ease back for a week before stepping up the intensity for the quarter-final and beyond. Training was lighter, the management team appeared notably calmer and, as we flew on to Brisbane, where we would play Uruguay, we were joined by the tour party of wives, children and girlfriends.

Unfortunately, Victoria wasn't among them. She was seven and a half months pregnant with our first child and, after weighing up the pros and cons, we decided it wouldn't be sensible for her to fly around the world in that condition. We spent many hours chatting on the telephone, but I still missed her terribly, particularly when the other guys started to spend most of their free time with their families and only a few of us were left on our own. Mark Regan and I tried to keep the coffee trips going, but we quickly realised spoof wasn't so much fun with only two people playing.

Boredom threatened, which meant I spent even longer on the telephone with Victoria, and the idea of taking up residence in one of the reclining seats around the hotel pool and soaking up some Brisbane sun began to seem appealing. Sadly, it wasn't an option because management had warned us about the debilitating effects of sunstroke and ruled that the players could not spend more than an hour in the baking sunshine each day.

This rule forced us to stay in the shade, mournfully looking out at the deep blue pool where Phil Larder and Dave Alred, two members of the coaching staff, were invariably to be found, sitting in their thongs, topping up their sunbed tans; and if they weren't there they were pushing weights in the gym. To be fair, both Phil and Dave were incredibly fit people, but the guys enjoyed ribbing them about the preening and posing by the pool.

Clive decided to give Gommers a start against Uruguay, and I was on the bench. Daws hadn't had a blinder against Western Samoa, so I was still hopeful of being the No. 1 scrum-half for the knockout stages. It was tight. Everything was in the balance, but getting a run and looking sharp in our last group game wasn't going to do my prospects any harm.

I felt calm and confident, and my back seemed to have settled down, but, in the event, the match was so one-sided that it didn't prove much to anyone. We won 111–13 and, although I did get on in the second half, most of us were left wondering about the point of the entire occasion. It's obviously important for the future of the game that lesser countries are encouraged and developed, but I'm not sure the World Cup is the right place to do it.

Mike Catt had a good day, proving his fitness and reminding everyone of his class. I congratulated him afterwards, and told him our decision to downplay our injuries at the start of the tour had been justified. Approaching the business end of the tournament, we were both challenging for a place in the starting XV.

That evening, we all gathered in the team room to watch the group match between Wales and New Zealand on television, aware we would meet the losers in the quarter-final. Everybody assumed that was going to be the Welsh but, in a World Cup with few shock results, we were amazed to see Wales playing all the rugby and deserving the lead they took into half time.

Nobody was too thrilled about the prospect of playing the

All Blacks in the quarter-final but, despite that, we were all supporting the Welsh because we were always going to get behind a European team trying to upset the Kiwis. Unfortunately, it didn't happen. The New Zealanders recovered and won the game, but we were left in no doubt that Wales were finding form at the right time and would provide serious opposition in the last eight.

Having won our group without ever having really shown our best form, we prepared for bigger challenges ahead.

'Feeling OK, KB?'

'Fine, just fine,' I told the coach, telling the truth.

I didn't know whether I would get a start against Wales. By general consent, I had done well against South Africa, and though Daws didn't have a great game against Samoa, it was never going to be a clear decision, but, to be honest, I was still disappointed when, at training on the Monday, Daws was given the bib for the team that was being lined up to play in the quarter-final.

I wanted to be the first choice. My back was fine and I felt sharp. On the other hand, after everything that had happened in the past year, recalling all the times when I had been on the brink of sitting at home, watching the World Cup on TV, I was still happy to be with the guys, and to be in the squad.

We prepared hard for the Welsh game, with Clive constantly warning us against complacency, but the knowledge that we had beaten them so regularly in recent years was difficult to set aside. Surely we had not come all this way to lose to Wales, we thought. Even if they do have a good spell, surely we'll be too strong. We knew that and we believed that and, no matter what anyone said, it was hard to shake off that kind of attitude.

At half time, we were losing 10–3. The fired-up Welsh pack had matched us in the set pieces and their efforts were rewarded when Stephen Jones, the Llanelli fly-half, scored the opening try of the quarter-final.

Some of the players on the bench were getting edgy but, to his credit, Clive kept his nerve and his decision to bring on Mike Catt as a substitute for Dan Luger, moving Mike Tindall to the wing, changed the course of the match and rescued the day. He quickly began to drive us forward with a series of long punts, and his solid, experienced presence at inside centre seemed to relieve the pressure on Jonny. It was almost as if Catty had started to tap out a beat, the rest of the team picked up the rhythm and we slowly ground out a 28–17 win.

'OK, we didn't play well,' Johnno said in the changing room afterwards, 'but we won, and that's what ******* matters. At the end of the day, it doesn't make any difference what anybody says about the way we play. If we win two more games, we're going to win this ******* World Cup. That's what counts.'

I had been given a run for the last quarter of an hour, as a sub for Daws, and made a few tackles, helping to nail down the victory, and those were highly significant minutes in my international rugby career because they secured my fiftieth cap for England. For some odd reason, that particular milestone had always seemed very important to me, and I was chuffed to have got there.

Over the years, whenever I sat down and contemplated what I wanted to achieve, I had always focused on the idea of winning fifty caps. Play for your country fifty times, I told myself, and then you will have had a successful career. It was not always about winning Grand Slams or even claiming the

World Cup. I always came back to this concept of playing fifty internationals for England.

This was a mistake. If I had put all my energies into being the first-choice scrum-half, I might well have achieved so much more. Instead, it was the target of fifty caps that drove me on, and, every time I was dropped, every time I was written off, every time I felt confidence draining away, I used to pick myself up by working out how many more caps I needed to reach fifty.

It didn't seem logical, but this mark became my Holy Grail and, sitting in the changing room after the World Cup quarter-final in Brisbane, I clasped it. I felt a fantastic sense of achievement. I had taken so many knocks along the way, but I had done it. It suddenly didn't matter what Stephen Jones wrote, and it didn't matter what Andy Robinson thought, I had got my fifty caps.

The guys were aware of my milestone after the Wales match, which I appreciated, and Johnno was especially kind, coming up to me, offering his congratulations and saying there weren't many who reached fifty caps. Daws was great as well. Coming from a guy who had been a huge rival, that meant a lot to me.

This was my mindset as we travelled to Sydney to prepare for the semi-final against France. I was sleeping well, my back felt fine, I was ready to give everything and, if called upon, I was eager to do my bit on the field, but, whatever happened, nobody was ever going to take away my fifty international caps for England.

We all knew the French were a genuine threat – in fact, they had been playing with such freedom that many people were saying they were the team of the tournament so far. So we trained hard, prepared carefully and respected them but, deep down, we also knew our recent results showed we could beat them.

At team meetings through the week, Johnno kept repeating that performances meant nothing as long as we were winning. We knew we were being criticised in the media, at home and in Australia, for not scoring enough tries and not being adventurous, but we didn't care so long as we kept winning, and we were determined we would not be upset or distracted by negative headlines.

For the first time, Clive was looking a bit edgy. He kept using the well-worn football manager's cliché about taking every match as it comes and, at one team meeting, he must have told us six or seven times he 'passionately believed' we would win the semi-final if we prepared like we did for any normal Test.

He was also getting animated about having so many wives and children around our hotel. Family were not allowed in the team room, and the coach kept saying that, although he 'trusted us all implicitly', this was not 'a holiday camp'. The wives and girlfriends didn't stay away, though; they just became more discreet, tiptoeing along the corridors, arriving and leaving by the back door.

My parents had flown out to watch the tournament, and they managed to book a room in the same Sydney hotel as us, which was perfect. Mum has always had a calming influence on me, and Dad is also completely supportive, quite apart from providing some serious opposition on the chessboard. Whenever I wanted a break from the team and all the rugby, I only had to nip up to their room, challenge Dad and immerse myself in chess.

John, my brother, had also said he would fly out to Australia if we reached the semi-finals, and he proved as good as his word. He got a room in the city centre and, in between having a beer with his mates, would catch the ferry across to Manly and see me between training and team meetings. If I couldn't have Victoria with me in Sydney, John was the next best thing. We are extremely close, and I have always felt able to confide in him.

Our tactics to beat France were simple: take them on up front, slow down their possession at set pieces, stop their offloads when they have the ball, cover their neat chip kicks over our defensive line, make sure we always find touch, never give them a platform to counterattack from deep and always, always build the score to gnaw away at their self-confidence and morale.

We also spent plenty of time planning how to stop the French half-backs from dominating the game. Fabien Galthié, their captain at nine, was adept at throwing brilliant dummies; and Frédéric Michalak was being eulogised as the best fly-half at the tournament, something that surely irritated Jonny.

I was picked among the substitutes in what was a predictable team selection, except for Clive's decision to start with Mike Catt at centre instead of Mike Tindall. Catty had been out of the Test side for a few years, but he had kept plugging away and, at thirty-two, was now a key part of our plans in a World Cup semi-final. When I told him that if he carried on like this he would make more comebacks than me, he said he didn't think that was possible.

On a wet evening when we really needed to be solid and professional, we were exactly that. The forwards swarmed over the French from the kick-off and, frankly, beat them up. We took charge in the set pieces and dominated the loose. In terms of intensity and discipline, it was our best performance of the tournament to date, and the French half-backs struggled: Galthié was given no room to create anything, and Michalak had a tough day.

As we moved further ahead in the second half, the guys on the subs' bench began to buzz. At last, things were going according to plan. At last, our hard work was paying off. At last, we looked like a team that could win the World Cup. It was great to watch, and all the subs were keen to get a run and really feel involved in the game. With ten minutes left, I was called on for Daws and, after putting in a couple of neat kicks and tackling Imanol Harinordoquy at the base of the scrum, I felt I had contributed to the 24–7 win.

Nobody was celebrating in our changing room after the game. There was a strange kind of calm as the players sat back, chilled out and nursed the various bumps and bruises. Everyone was unmistakably pleased, but we hadn't won anything yet. 'Well done, lads,' Johnno said, not for the first time perfectly assessing the mood of his side. 'Now, let's save the partying until after the final.'

Back at our hotel, after chatting on the phone to Victoria, I met up with my family and, over a few drinks, played a Tri-Nations chess tournament between my dad, my brother and me. Together with Mum, we talked long into the night, telling and retelling all the old stories from when John and I were kids. It felt good to be with them all, and it felt good to be in the World Cup final.

Blackpool had come to Sydney.

Through the week leading to the final, the area around our hotel in particular seemed to be constantly packed with thousands and thousands of England fans who had flown around the world in the hope of seeing their team win a

World Cup for the first time since 1966. Every face seemed to be burned lobster red, the beer flowed and flags of St George fluttered in every direction.

The level of support was fantastic, even though it turned our lives into a bit of a circus. It soon became obvious that, as players, it was becoming impossible for us to set foot outside the hotel without being mobbed by well-meaning people who wanted us to autograph a T-shirt or just to have a chat. Even as we were leaving for training, huge crowds cheered us onto the team bus. Going out for a quiet coffee was out of the question and when some of the players went to eat at a restaurant, they had to leave before their food came because the crowds were getting out of hand.

In the end, we just stayed inside the hotel, feeling imprisoned by the enthusiasm and sheer numbers of our own supporters. When the weather was good, most of us longed to hit the beach and go swimming in the ocean, until we remembered what had happened to some of the players, who had yielded to the temptation, gone for a surf and been reprimanded by our management. While everyone else was getting into party mode, we needed to focus on the rugby.

Our opponents in the final were the Australians, who, slightly against the odds, had beaten the All Blacks 22–10 in the semi-final the day before our match. Nobody had rated the Wallabies in the run-up to the World Cup but, typically, they had produced a big performance on another big occasion and, all of a sudden, they were one home final away from being World Champions for the third time.

Even on TV, we could see the New Zealanders were absolutely shattered in defeat. They had many great players but, once again, they had promised so much and delivered so little. Their undoing was possibly the decision to play without an established and reliable goal-kicker. While Carlos Spencer is a brilliant fly-half, he very rarely kicks well under pressure. A goal-kicker like Jonny, with a constant success rate of 90 per cent, is an incredible asset. Some people say he's worth a fifteen-point start, and I don't disagree.

Our only selection issue before the final seemed to concern the midfield combination, and this time Clive opted to prefer the direct, sheer physicality of Mike Tindall ahead of Catty's guile and experience. It seemed the right decision because we wanted to run straight at the Wallabies and, if we did need stability at any stage, it would be easy to summon Mike Catt from the bench.

Clive could see the players were tired after three tough matches on successive weekends, so our training before the final was lighter than usual, with a series of short, sharp sessions rather than endurance exercises that would sap the muscles. Above all, everybody was determined to avoid getting any kind of injury in a stupid training-ground accident, and risk missing the final. In this regard, two unfortunate incidents earlier in the tour persuaded some of the guys that I was a danger.

First, holding a bag during tackling practice, I had managed to give Catty whiplash. I caught him square in the neck and he fell to the ground, screaming in agony. My first thought was that Catty had broken his neck, and the coaches wanted to call an ambulance. In the end he was driven to hospital, where X-rays showed no real damage, but he didn't feel well for several days.

I apologised to Mike, and felt terrible . . . at least until I took out Iain Balshaw on the training field and had to concentrate on feeling sorry for him. We were trying to defend a two-on-one situation, so I shouted for him to push out. He did, but I lost my balance, tripped and collided into him. When I looked up, Iain was writhing around in agony. He was taken to hospital, where doctors found a small tear in the ankle ligament and ruled him out for a week.

Iain joked that he would sue me for compensation if he had to be sent home, so I was every bit as relieved as him when he made a full recovery and resumed training. 'Keep away from KB if you want to stay fit,' he warned the others.

The level of excitement, and probably intoxication, among our supporters built steadily through the week, and it had reached what seemed ludicrous proportions by the time we were leaving the hotel for our last training session on the Friday morning. As soon as the team bus pulled up outside the hotel door, ready to drive us to the field, thousands of England fans began to gather, hoping for a quick glimpse of the players as we walked past.

When we eventually emerged from the hotel, the crowd went mad. We were a bunch of rugby players suddenly being treated like pop stars, and it felt quite bizarre. The most deafening roars were reserved for the three 'superstars' in the squad – Jonny, Johnno and Clive – and each of them responded typically.

Jonny looked at the ground, clearly embarrassed by the sight of hysterical girls yelling his name, Johnno looked straight ahead, resolutely focused on the job at hand, and Clive looked all around, smiling and waving regally at the crowd. The guys were excited, joking, lapping up the crazy experience, and some of us thought the coach was being a bit cocky, so he took some flak.

Even when everyone was aboard and we drove away to training, we looked back to see half a dozen fans sprinting after the bus, holding cameras, trying to get another photo.

A few moments later, we saw a group of young lads in Australian shirts, standing in a line on a wall. As our bus passed, they all turned around, dropped their trousers and started slapping their arses. Everybody laughed at this performance but, as someone said, we had to make sure it was us slapping their arses in the final the next day.

When we arrived at the training ground, there were more fans waiting to meet us, including a group of schoolgirls who appeared to be playing truant. Clive had told us to be careful where we signed autographs for young girls, particularly when we were asked to put our signatures anywhere near the bosom area. We all listened to this advice, and then took great delight in ignoring it. Everyone was having a good time and the mood was great.

We usually trained at the stadium on the day before a Test match but, on this particular occasion, we just headed for a training field near the hotel. The players didn't enjoy the long bus drive to the Telstra Stadium, and had said so, and, in any case, we knew what to expect because we had played there the previous Sunday. Not for the first time, management listened to our views and arrived at what seemed a sensible decision.

Even though we were training at a standard club ground in a Sydney suburb, the venue was thoroughly prepared. Clive remained adamant about the issue of security and the field had clearly been chosen with this in mind. We noticed how, to be doubly certain of our privacy, yards of thick, black tape had been used to block out gaps in the perimeter fence. It must have taken several days to set up but, in this campaign, it seemed someone had thought of everything.

The changing room at the field had also been set up in a way that we all recognised. Familiarity bred confidence, and it was good to see tables laden with nutritional, protein-filled foods and fluids and, most popular of all, the sweets box. We were only allowed to eat sweets before and after training sessions and, of all the kinds, the long jelly snakes were invariably the first to go.

Friday training sessions are usually exercises in fine-tuning, a bit of running to loosen the joints and ease the nerves, followed by a few line-out drills for the forwards and some rehearsal of moves for the backs, but today the management kept the running to a minimum because they wanted us to stay fresh. More quickly than usual, we were divided into forwards and backs.

Clive oversaw the backs and seemed surprisingly relaxed on the eve of such a massive game, while Robbo took the pack through some line-out drills, growling at anyone who made a mistake. Long after we had returned to the changing room, and the sweets box, the harassed forwards were still being pushed to get the right lift or a perfectly timed jump. We didn't envy them.

I practised a few extra passes just to stay neat and sharp but, as I knew as well as anyone, preparing to be a substitute in such a huge match was always hard. You feel more relaxed than the guys in the starting XV, but there's always a thought nagging at the back of your mind that something might just happen and you could find yourself being summoned in the first few minutes. That had never happened to me, but there was always a first. In the end, you just get yourself ready and take whatever happens.

Before long, we were back on the bus, waiting to head back to the hotel, but Jonny and the other kickers had decided to stay at the field and practise their goal-kicking. It was at this point that a helicopter appeared overhead, carrying a photographer who clearly began taking pictures of Jonny in training. These photos were doubtless going to be splashed over the next day's newspapers because they would effectively support the Australian media's portrayal of the England team as Dad's Army relying almost completely on a goal-kicking machine.

Nobody minded either the image or the helicopter, least of all Jonny, who by now was resolutely focused on one of his favourite kicking drills, where he set up the ball on the try-line and aimed to hit the side of the goalpost. I was amazed at how often he struck the five-inch target, and reckoned it was no wonder he made firing the ball in the space between the posts look so easy.

The main topic of conversation at the rear of the bus on the drive back to our hotel was the exchange of text messages that appeared to have taken place between Clive and Lawrence Dallaglio earlier that morning. Rugby players love a good story as much as anyone, and nothing stays secret for very long on tour.

According to the grapevine, which was not always completely reliable, this was the story. Each morning we would have breakfast together in the hotel dining room, so there were often members of the public around, but today Lawrence had come down, met some of his family friends and had breakfast with them. Clive arrived soon afterwards, saw Lol and gave him the evil eye.

The No. 8 subsequently received a text message from the coach about this, concerned that there was a possibility that he might be getting distracted from the job in hand. Lol was very irritated by this and apparently tapped back an angry message confirming that he was entirely focused on winning the World Cup.

It was all good stuff, and it kept everybody nattering until we pulled up outside our hotel, where the crowd of supporters seemed to have been waiting for a couple of hours in the sun just to watch us walk a few yards from the bus to the main door. They went crazy again, chanting Johnno's name, and although they were clearly disappointed when they saw Jonny wasn't with us on the bus, Clive was there, giving them his customary wave.

Into the afternoon, with any venture beyond the hotel out of the question, the players again lost themselves in what had become the extremely familiar routine of eating sandwiches in the team room, watching videos, playing golf on the PlayStation and chatting. We had been living through the same Groundhog Day for the past two months, but it was coming to an end.

I sat there and thought it was surprising that nobody seemed to be showing any sign of nerves. We were just twenty-four hours from the World Cup final, yet everyone seemed focused and calm, maybe a little quieter than usual, but not much. We had trained so hard, and prepared so thoroughly, it almost seemed as though each of us had subconsciously switched onto a kind of autopilot. We knew exactly what we had to do, and we were ready to do it.

A team meeting had been called for six o'clock in the evening and, as all the players looked forward to the inspiring video montage and a couple of rousing speeches from Clive and Johnno, Mark Regan and I took a side bet on how many times the coach would repeat the phrase 'I passionately believe we can win this'. I guessed he would say it three times, Mark went for four, and we both waited anxiously to see who would be proved right.

The video was brilliant. We were used to watching a

different one before every international, and the guys really enjoyed them, but we were really moved and inspired by the clever combination of triumphant images from our matches on the way to the final and some shots of us working hard in training.

Clive spoke next, reminding us how we had one opportunity and there would be no second chance. We might have laughed at him now and then, as every group of players laughs at every coach, but he had earned our complete respect over the years. Most of us had come a long way with him and now, on the brink of achieving our ultimate goal, his words were received in silence. However, on this occasion, Clive did repeat his catchphrase about 'passionately believing we could win' no fewer than four times, triggering ecstatic, if necessarily silent, celebrations by Mark Regan, sitting beside me at the back of the room.

Then it was Johnno's turn to speak, and he just sat there for a few seconds, looking around at his team. He waited for complete silence, before speaking bluntly, in his own way.

I didn't write down what the captain said, but it was a great speech, and it ran something like this: 'Let's get into these ******* right from the off. They have spouted off some **** in these past few weeks, so let's shut them up in the first minute. We have won here before and we'll do it again.

'It's just another game. Don't get lost in the fact that it's the World Cup final. It's eighty minutes of fifteen against fifteen, and we want it more than them. Work rate! Work rate! Work rate. When we feel tired, we get off the floor and make our tackles.'

Johnno was getting us all worked up, and as I looked around the room I thought it was a pity we couldn't go out and take on the Australians there and then, but he finished calmly. 'OK, guys,' he said almost softly, 'let's save it for tomorrow night.'

Then, as usual on the nights before internationals, most of us stayed in the team room and played 'the name game', where you were given two letters in the alphabet and had to come up with the name of a well-known person. For example, if the letters were 'J' and 'W', your answer could be Jonny Wilkinson.

You lost points if the name had been mentioned before, and you earned extra points if you thought of a name from a nominated category, like film stars or cartoon characters. Martin Johnson, Will Greenwood and Ben Kay were regular winners but, more often than not, I was rubbish and soon lost interest.

That night, we watched a film in the team room, and ate more food, more sandwiches, protein shakes and popcorn, and at around half past nine I nipped off to my parents' room for another game of chess with my dad. He beat me in just fifteen moves.

I was in my own room by eleven and, after calling Victoria, lay in bed, looking at the sleeping tablets on the table beside my bed. I decided I wouldn't need them, turned over, closed my eyes and, thankfully, on this night of all nights, drifted off to sleep.

CHAPTER TWO

A bleary glance at my watch tells me it's shortly after one o'clock in the morning, which means I must have slept for two hours. Now it's 22 November, my birthday, the day of the Rugby World Cup final, a big day in every respect. I look at the sleeping tablets on the bedside table. I still don't need them. I feel fine. I might have woken in the middle of the night, but I'm not anxious or feeling the pressure. This isn't insomnia; it's excitement. I'm like the kid before Christmas, buzzing, impatient, eager to see what tomorrow brings. In twenty hours, we'll be into the match, bidding for glory, giving everything. I can hardly wait.

The TV remote control is close at hand and I indifferently flick through the channels, until I settle on a rerun of a sports talk show where Australian pundits are indulging in Pombashing. I watch for a minute and then tap the off button. They can be as brash as they like, I tell myself; we'll take them in the final.

What now? What about my kit? When you play for

England, most of your playing kit is provided and laid out in the changing room when you arrive at the stadium, but I get up and take care to check my boots are clean and my gumshield is OK. I don't want to forget anything or make any mistakes, not today. My formal wear looks all right. The official light grey suit is hanging on the cupboard door with the light blue shirt and the red tie, and the brown shoes are clean. Everything is fine. I check it all once, then check it again, and check it a third time.

The calls? What about the calls? It's generally much harder to remember all the calls when you are a substitute, because you don't get the opportunity to run through everything in training. You just watch, and try to learn everything off paper. So I decide I should study the calls again because, if I do get on the field, I can't afford to make any mistakes, not in the final.

I still remember the afternoon before the 2003 Six Nations match against Wales in Cardiff. I had been allocated a hotel room next to Jonny Wilkinson and, when I stepped onto the balcony of my room, I could actually see straight into his room. Each time I looked during a period of two or three hours I saw him deep in thought, writing notes, learning the moves and studying the game plan. You get out of this game what you are prepared to put in. So I sit on the bed and read through pages of moves and calls.

Minutes pass like hours. My sister Jane and her husband David are scheduled to arrive in Sydney tomorrow afternoon. Jane had always promised she would fly over if we reached the final and, somehow, she managed to get a seat on the packed flights from London. She will spend only eleven hours in Australia, sandwiched between a total travelling time of fifty-six hours. That's what I call real

Standing proudly with my slide at home in Ireland.

The four Bracken children, Jane, John, me and Louise, get ready to wave the flags when the Queen visited Liverpool.

On tour with Stonyhurst in Sydney in 1989, before the players from St Ignatius' College got hold of me.

Shaking hands with
David Humphries
after the England v
Ireland Schoolboy
international in 1989.

With Alastair Hignell
(left) and Bob Reeves,
the Bristol University
coach who taught me
so much.

In action for Bristol University in March 1993 in the UAU final against
Loughborough at Twickenham. (*Colorsport*)

Top Getting the ball away quickly as Richard Hill of Bath watches on in the Bristol–Bath derby on 31 October 1992, during my first season for the club. When one or two of the Bath players tried to put the cocky young student in his place, I was very relieved to have forwards like Alan Sharp to protect me. (*Colorsport*)

Bottom Another game against Bath, another painful experience. This time Andy Robinson helps grind me into the mud. The bandage round his head came when two of my teeth got embedded in his head. (*Colorsport*)

KYRAN BRACKEN

Soon after making my debut for England I got lots of offers to do modelling, and I certainly enjoyed the opportunities that came my way – as long as I could keep my clothes on!

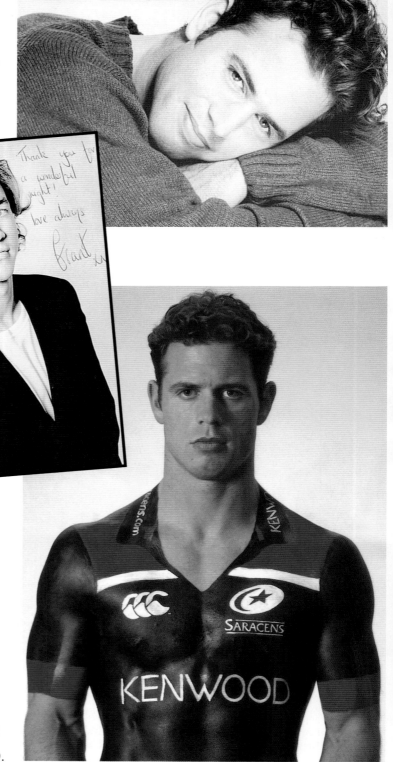

Thank you for a wonderful night! love always

Grant xx

Grant

Grant Bulstrode, a former team-mate at Bristol, gained access to my flat when they were filming *Through the Keyhole* and left this photo in a prominent position.

Wearing the painted shirt of the Saracens (*Action Images*).

August 1996: Michael Lynagh, Philippe Sella and I join Saracens at the start of the first season of professional club rugby. (*Getty Images*)

Right Nigel Wray, the man who has put so much money into Saracens and has been such a loyal supporter of rugby. (*David Rogers/Getty Images*)

Scoring a try for the Lions during my only appearance for the side, against Northern Free State in July 1997. I dislocated my AC shoulder joint in doing so. (*Empics*)

Leaving Northampton scrum-half Matt Dawson in my wake. Although we have long been rivals for the England No. 9 shirt, we are also good mates. (*Colorsport*)

Caught again by Danny Grewcock. He may be one of my best friends, but he has caused me all sorts of pain on – and off – the rugby field. (*Colorsport*)

Opposite

Top Racing for the line on our way to beating Wasps in the Tetley's Bitter Cup final of 1998. My opposite number can't hold on to me. (*Action Plus*)

Inset Francois Pienaar holds aloft the trophy after our 48–18 victory. (*Getty Images*)

Bottom The celebrations begin on the best day I've ever had in club rugby. (*Colorsport*)

Victoria and I on our wedding day on 22 July 2001.

With Victoria, the love of my life.

Little Charlie, aged eight months who has put rugby into a proper perspective for me.

commitment to me, her brother, to my cause. I get a lump in my throat. We'd better win.

When she gets here, we'll have five of the six Bracken family members in one place, with only my sister Louise missing. It's a shame she couldn't be here as well, but she's just got married and work commitments have prevented it. That will be great because we have always been a very close family. In good times and bad times, they have been so supportive of me and my rugby. All said and done, they have shaped me.

For example, I believe the intensely competitive nature of my relationship with my older brother, John, ever since we were kids, has been directly responsible for the fanatical determination to win that has propelled me through my rugby career. As the third of four children, I felt I had to fight for every bit of attention and advantage, and John, always just a bit older and a bit bigger, became my yardstick. Whatever game we were playing, whatever we were doing, I simply had to be better than John, just had to beat John. It was war.

Whenever I lost, which was most of the time because I would usually get muscled out of the game, I would run away to a quiet corner of the house and sit, crying my eyes out, promising myself that one day, when I was stronger, I would attack him and beat him up once and for all. Fortunately, this 'fight to end all fights' never happened. We have always got along well.

I hated losing to John, and have hated losing ever since. I desperately wanted to beat him . . . and at school and at university I became obsessed with winning every game. I couldn't stand the idea of John ever being better than me . . . even now, I hate to think anyone is better than me. As I

played in the back garden, so I have played my rugby career
... ready to do anything, train the hardest, and practise the
longest, just to win.

Of course, the truth is I idolised John and have done for as
long as I can remember, and, even if I would never have
admitted it at the time, I wanted to be just like him. When I
was seven, he was nine. When I was nine, he was eleven.
Looking back, I seem to have spent most of my childhood
trying to match John, trying to catch up with John, trying to
be like John. Simply by being there, always ahead, he drove
me to realise my potential.

If anyone asks who has had the greatest influence on me,
in rugby and in life, I don't hesitate to say my brother. That's
not only because he put up with me for so long, always
playing with me even when I behaved so badly if things
didn't go my way. It's also because, in subsequent years, John
has always loved my success, helped me in hard times and
never been jealous.

My childhood was happy, even if I never saw the silver
spoon that Austin Healey insists was stuck in my mouth
when I was born, on 22 November 1971, in Ireland. Mum
and Dad were childhood sweethearts from Skerries, a small
fishing village up the coast from Dublin. Dad was a dentist
and Mum was a PE teacher, who played hockey for Ireland
until, in her first match, she was nearly blinded by a stray
German stick and then had to retire.

As parents, they were hard and fair. We never had the
latest Atari video games or trendy clothes, but we had what
we needed. We never jetted to the Caribbean, but we went
camping in France, where we battled to read the road signs,
got lost and generally seemed to pitch the tent on an anthill.
We were never given fistfuls of fivers to spend, but we could

earn our pocket money by cleaning the car, pruning the roses or weeding the garden.

I suppose four children born within the space of five years were always likely to fight, and we did, but we rarely overstepped the mark. One time, my parents went skiing for a week and left us with a minder. The day before they got home, John and I found the keys to the bar and, together with a friend of mine, we started to drink a few cocktails. We were playing around, but my friend got stuck into the Baileys and my parents arrived back to find him unconscious on the living-room floor.

He had his stomach pumped and spent a few days in hospital, which seemed like fun compared to our fate. John and I were given a good, old-fashioned, wholly deserved beating, after which we hid under the stairs for several hours, swearing we would run away and become professional rugby league players. Back then, there seemed no better life than being paid to play rugby.

It was Dad who had decided we should leave Ireland, because he saw an opportunity to open his own dental practice in England. So when I was three, against the wishes of our relations, the Brackens moved to Liverpool. Mum missed her family and took time to settle, but before too long Dad's practice was thriving and the four of us were running around talking like little Scousers.

My parents didn't like our accents, and we used to tease them that that was why they sent us to smart schools. In fact, education has always been important to Irish Catholic families like ours, and Mum and Dad made huge sacrifices to pay the fees and send us to the best schools in the area. John and I went to St Edward's, and Louise and Jane were sent to the local convent school.

We messed around with kids in our neighbourhood, which was close enough to Toxteth to be affected by the rioting of the early 1980s, and rough enough for Mum's car to keep being stolen; once it was used in an armed raid and returned the next day. We got up to all kinds of mischief, but somehow managed to stay out of real trouble until a teachers' strike created problems for us in 1983.

While most kids were off school and hanging around the streets, the fee-paying schools stayed open and we became sitting targets, continuing to travel to and from St Edward's in our purple blazers. One afternoon, John and I, and a few friends, were joined on the No. 59 bus to Rainhill by around thirty or forty bored kids from the West Derby Comprehensive, with nothing better to do than pick a fight. We quickly took off our distinctive blazers, trying to hide them from view, but we were not going to escape.

The taunting soon started, and an uncomfortable situation got worse when one kid slapped me across the head from behind. He was much older, bigger and stronger than any of us, but John was always protective of his younger brother, so he stood up and spat in my attacker's eye and then, while the kid wiped the spittle from his face, followed up with a crunching head-butt. The kid hit the deck and stayed there. His nose was gushing blood, but the bus suddenly went quiet and we didn't get any more hassle.

John wasn't always there to look after me. Another day, I was walking out of school alone when a kid approached me and asked if I had a light. I said no. He then wanted some money for a bus fare and, while I was looking for coins, he smacked me in the face. I went down and saw his mates surrounding me. They were stronger and bigger than me, like opposing props in days to come, but I thought I was faster, so I got to my feet and ran away. They gave chase and, in what was starting to look like a scene from a gangland movie, I decided my only hope was to jump into the passenger seat of a car waiting outside the school. The mother was surprised, but I shouted at her to drive and when she saw my assailants approaching she took me to safety.

Life was never dull in Liverpool, but we all loved the city. The humour, the spirit and the sense of community were fantastic, and before long we couldn't imagine living anywhere else, even though our immigrant status meant we got abuse on both side of the Irish Sea. Our mates in Liverpool generally called us 'Paddies', but, when we went to visit our relations back in Ireland, they took delight in dismissing us as a bunch of 'English tossers'.

Sport was always part of our family life. Mum took the girls to lacrosse and horse riding, and Dad used to drive John and me all over the region for football and rugby. Football was initially my preferred sport and one day I scored three goals in a final trial for Liverpool FC schoolboys, but this was the era of hooliganism and the Heysel tragedy, and Dad was keen for me to play rugby. There were days when he refused to drive me to football practice, forcing me to go to rugby training instead. I used to get so angry with him but, looking back, it's pretty obvious he made the right call.

John and I dabbled with junior rugby league at St Helens, but we eventually ended up playing the union game at Waterloo RFC, a great club with a terrific atmosphere where we both made lifelong friends. Dad was always there, and I remember he used to say that top players could pass and kick on both sides. Most youngsters used only their 'good' side, but Dad was insistent and he actually banned me from using my naturally favoured right side. I played like an idiot for a while, as I learned to kick and pass on my left, but I soon got the hang of it and today I reckon I am stronger and more consistent on my left than on my natural right.

One year, our Under-13 team was sent away to a five-day preseason training camp at Trent College. I was excited and we trained really hard, but everything turned sour when we managed to get served at the local pub, got plastered, got caught and were frogmarched into an office the next morning.

'You're going to be sent home,' the college administrator told us, 'and none of you will ever play representative rugby.' We all felt completely devastated. His name was Mike Slemen, the former international wing who, strangely, would later be my back-line coach in the England squad. Whenever I was dropped from the national team, I used to tease Mike that it was only because he still blamed me for the teenage drinking all those years before.

I also got involved in other sports, like tennis, which I enjoyed and did quite well, and cross-country running, which I hated and, unfortunately, also did quite well. I generally came in the top five or six until, one day, Dad promised me a can of Coke if I finished first. There were plenty of hills on the course, which suited me, and I managed to win. I will never forget the feeling of complete delight when my dad walked up and presented me with a six-pack of Coca-Cola.

Every summer, I spent most of my time on athletics, mainly the 100 metres sprint but, oddly, I also did quite well in the discus, and managed to qualify for the national schools championships when I was fifteen. This proved to be a terrifying experience. I arrived on the day of the event and immediately realised that, in a group of about thirty throwers, I was not only a foot shorter than anyone else but also the only one who hadn't started to shave.

My unease was compounded when it became clear that I was the only competitor who spun around before making my throw. The others just stood there, but they still hurled the discus further than me and, predictably, I finished stone last. Concluding what was a less than glorious day, my parents had hit traffic on their way to the venue and arrived moments after my last throw.

At least they were prepared to make an eight-hour round trip to get there at all. Mum and Dad were always there for all of us, encouraging their four children, equally, in whatever we tried to do, committing themselves to giving us the best chance of being successful, driving all over the country to drop us here or there, endlessly. They were firm when necessary, but always supportive.

It may be an old cliché, but the four of us simply would not be where we are today without their help. Louise and Jane are both in Jersey, working as a chartered accountant and an endodontist, a specialist dentist, respectively. John is a property developer and, apart from my rugby, I also have a legal background. I hope my parents are proud.

It has become an old family joke that even after sending all his children to fee-paying primary schools, even after banning them all from watching *Brookside*, the Merseyside TV soap opera, my dad still thought we sounded like Scouse scallywags, so he forked out more cash and sent his sons to boarding school.

In fact, he simply wanted us to have the best education his hard-earned money could buy. First John, then I, following two years later, was packed off to Stonyhurst College, in Lancashire, a Roman Catholic school founded in 1593 and effectively run by Jesuit priests, reputed to be stricter than strict. We were being rigorously prepared for adult life, but Mum cried every time she came to the school, and she only had to stay a few hours.

Both John and I initially found it hard to adapt. We may have seemed well off in the area of Liverpool where we lived, but we felt a little out of place among the plummy accents and wealth of the other boys at Stonyhurst. About the only thing we had in common with them was that they didn't watch *Brookside* either. In any case, we jumped in with both feet and soon settled.

Boarding school seems to suit some and haunt others. Many of the kids had been sent away from home when they were just six or seven, which seemed a bit harsh, but I was packed off at the age of thirteen and I enjoyed every minute of it. The spirit, the routine, the mates and, of course, the sport suited me down to the ground and, after a while, I even got used to the discipline.

John didn't always find the Stonyhurst lifestyle so easy and one evening he was caught sneaking away from school for a couple of beers and a smoke. The teachers instructed him to say who else was involved but, being a loyal kind of guy, John refused to squeal on his mates, even though that resolve meant he was suspended from school for ten days, instead of only six.

Unfortunately, my parents were away when all this happened and, in their absence, the school decided John should serve out his suspension isolated and alone in the infirmary. It's hard to believe what my brother suffered: his only form of exercise came when he was driven to a point five miles away and told to run back to the school; his only contact with anyone else was a daily visit from me when I took him his homework, but even then we were not allowed to speak a single word to each other. Tears used to well in my eyes when I saw John like that, caged and miserable.

My parents went absolutely berserk when they returned and discovered how their son had been treated, and it was probably a blessing for all concerned when John left Stonyhurst after sitting his O levels, even though I missed his company. By then, my family had moved from Liverpool to settle in Jersey, and John had a great time completing his education on the island.

I probably enjoyed Stonyhurst so much because I managed to get into most of the sports teams. It certainly wasn't because I was a sensation in the classroom, where six Bs and one C in my GCSE exams left me looking pretty ordinary. When the teachers predicted I would end up with B, C, C in my three A levels (History, Ancient History and Philosophy), that old Irish stubbornness kicked in, and I decided it was just about time to start working.

Brian Ashton, one of my teachers, who ironically would later coach the England rugby team, helped by moving me into a brighter set, and I responded by studying from six in the morning until after midnight almost every day for four months. The results were two As and a C in my A levels, which surprised everyone and didn't seem too bad for a little Scouser like me.

Rugby is traditionally important at Stonyhurst and I benefited from the outstanding coaching and facilities, so much so that I was included in the England Schools side a year young in 1988–89, and then captained the team in the following season. Such status was a fantastic confidence boost, but it set me up for a hard fall when the Stonyhurst first XV went on a world tour in 1990.

Our itinerary took us through Los Angeles, Australia, Fiji and Singapore, with our toughest match being against the renowned St Ignatius' College, a sister school of Stonyhurst in Sydney. They hosted a dinner for us on the night before the game, where we made the grave mistake of identifying those of us who had played for England Schools. We may as well have had blood daubed on our foreheads because, during the match, each of us internationals was targeted and forced to leave the field with a serious injury. My nose was smashed, fractured in three places, and had to be reconstructed when we got home to England.

Needless to say, we lost the game and weren't too happy with our opponents afterwards but, even then, I had a grudging respect for the St Ignatius' boys, which in seasons to come would extend to the Wallabies. Whatever you say about Australians, they are tough competitors. They seem to have an aura of invincibility, sustained by massive self-confidence and an amazing will to win, and losing to Aussies was a regular feature of my career ... until we finally started to turn the tables, when victory tasted all the sweeter.

So I left Stonyhurst with many happy memories. Like many institutions, it has endured problems in recent years, but it remains a great school, going from strength to strength, and I will always be proud to be a former pupil.

My original plan was to move on and study Ancient History at Bristol University, but the decent A level results seemed to have raised the bar, and Dad suddenly started talking about reading Law at Oxford. He said a top degree like that would be a licence to make money, a remark that successfully attracted my attention, but I had set my mind on going to Bristol and suggested I still do that, but try to change courses from Ancient History to Law.

Dad thought that was OK but, in the meantime, without even telling me, he applied to Oxford on my behalf. So, completely out of the blue, I received a letter from Oxford asking me to explain why I wanted to do Law. Well, I had no idea, so I got a friend to write me a fantastic letter, so convincing I had to add a few spelling mistakes to make it realistic, and waited for the response.

A few days later, Dad came bounding up, saying the Head of Faculty of Law at Oxford was going to phone me later that day and ask some questions about Contract law. He explained it would be a kind of telephonic interview. I panicked because I knew very little indeed about Contract law, and sprinted down to the local library to swot on some law books. A few hours later, I returned home to find the rest of my family rolling around in fits of laughter.

'Nobody's going to call you,' Dad said, grinning. 'Oxford have offered you a place, on condition you take a year off.'

It was incredible news. I was amazed, and flattered, but still not sure whether I had the confidence to mix with the great and the good at Oxford, and, in any case, I didn't really want to take a year off. After some discussion, when Bristol confirmed I could switch my course to Law everyone agreed that option would suit me best. Dad didn't mind too much, and it proved a great decision.

Bristol University was a blast, from start to finish. On the first night of the first term of my first year, a group of us got together in one lad's room and, as the beers came out, which was a sign of things to come, I met a guy called Simon Aired. We started chatting about rugby, and he said he was a scrum-half.

'So am I,' I replied.

'Pity,' Simon said. 'You'll have no chance of getting into the university team because, apparently, the England Schools captain is coming. He's called Kyran Bracken, and he's a little tosser. They say he's a decent player, but he loves himself.'

'Oh,' I said.

Simon didn't realise he was talking to the 'little tosser' himself until much later in the evening, and he looked horrified for a moment, but we all laughed and moved right through three years at university together. In my first year, there was scarcely an evening when we didn't go out somewhere for a drink.

The Head of Physical Education at Bristol was Bob Reeves, a talented, dedicated man who had already helped me by arranging what was the first sports scholarship ever offered by Bristol. The sum of £500 per year may not seem huge now, but it made a massive difference to a youthful student like me. Bob became a firm friend, and he always had my best interests at heart.

Once a week, along with several other sportsmen and women, I used to go to the Sports Faculty for a two-hour session where we spoke about improving performance. We ran through the normal stuff about setting short-term and long-term goals, and looked at other disciplines and, although it sometimes felt like a chore at the time, I later realised this kind of thinking and coaching gave me an important head start against most of my rivals.

Simon Aired's prediction did come true in my first year, when I was chosen for the university rugby team, although I nearly didn't get much further than the induction. Each new player was forced to down three pints of 'Snakebite and

Black' (a cloudy blend of lager, cider and blackcurrant cordial), and they had to drink it from a funnel that was held high up against the ceiling so that the evil mixture reached your stomach in about three seconds.

I thought I was a bit of a lad in those days and could cope with anything out of a bottle, but I was soon so drunk that, faced by the next stage of the induction, having to smash a glass on top of my own head, I missed the target and cut my forehead. Blood gushed all over the place, which was pretty embarrassing, but at least I was left with a small, neat scar that, even today, stands as testament to my induction into the Bristol University Rugby Club.

Student life soon settled into a happy routine. Law proved a tough course, and I was kept busy attending lectures, writing essays and keeping up with my studies, but each week really revolved around rugby, on and off the field. We used to play on Wednesday afternoons and hit the beers together after the game. Then we would play again on Saturday and return to the same familiar bars that night. We trained hard, performed well and revelled in the team spirit.

Today, I look at younger players coming into the game and I feel they miss out in so many ways. Most of them are eager to sign professional contracts with a senior club at eighteen and make a full-time commitment to the game, but it seems to me that (1) this means they don't finish a proper education, so they often have no career to fall back on after rugby; (2) they don't get much chance to mix with their own age group and do the normal student things; and (3) they actually don't play that much rugby because there will usually be an international player occupying their position in the first team.

Given the opportunity to turn professional at eighteen, I

would have jumped at the chance but, with hindsight, I am very pleased I never had that option. Instead, between the ages of eighteen and twenty-one, at Bristol, I somehow completed a 2:1 Law degree, had a great time with my mates and played loads of competitive rugby.

I was very fortunate, and I owe a great deal to Bob Reeves, who guided me through this period, encouraging me to complete my degree and stopping me from playing senior club rugby until my final year. In essence, he helped me make the right decisions when it would have been easy to spin off the rails. So I kept playing for the university and loved every minute, particularly our run in the 1993 UAU tournament, a knockout event for the university teams in Britain, when we progressed to the final and played against Loughborough at Twickenham.

We had scraped through the semi-final against Durham when, leading by two points in the last minute of the game, we conceded a penalty in front of our own posts. Tim Stimpson, who would later be an England team-mate of mine, just had to kick the penalty for them and we were out but, thinking we led by four points, he took a tap and ran for the line. We stopped him short and, as the final whistle blew, the Durham players stared at Tim in disbelief. It was a bizarre moment, but Tim came through it, played many great games for club and country, and, nine years on, kicked a last-minute penalty from halfway, bouncing on the bar and over, to carry Leicester to a European Cup semi-final victory over Llanelli.

Riding our luck, we were not given much chance in the final against mighty Loughborough, who included several capped players, such as the huge Welsh lock, Derwyn Jones. Grant Bulstrode, one of my closest friends, was given the task of marking Jones in the line-outs and, before the game, he boasted how he had a great plan to prevent Jones from dominating the match. When we asked him to explain his idea, he told us to wait and see.

We didn't have to be patient for long. Just as the first line-out of the final was being formed, Grant stepped across and gave the 6' 10" second-row forward a big kiss on the lips. Derwyn went crazy and a big fight broke out. The referee calmed things down, but he burst out laughing when Derwyn complained that a Bristol player had kissed him. We got the penalty and, with a bit of guts, managed to harass and hassle the favourites out of their stride.

The scores were level at the end of normal time and it seemed as if we might cause an upset, but this particular Cinderella wasn't going to get to the ball ... Tony Diprose, the Loughborough captain and later my team-mate for Saracens and England, did, plunging to score a winning pushover try in the last minute of extra time.

When Bob Reeves felt the time was right, in 1992, my last year at university, he introduced me to Rob Cunningham, the Bristol RFC first-team coach. As a carefree student, with a relaxed outlook on life and extravagantly long curly hair, I prepared for my baptism into senior club rugby.

'Oy! That's my peg,' said Alan Sharp, a prop, as he took my clothes down and threw them on the changing-room floor. Arriving for my first training session with Bristol, I had casually taken the peg nearest the door. That was clearly a mistake. The players didn't much like 'cocky students' at the best of times, and I had appeared to fit the stereotype. So, feeling foolish, I gathered up my clothes and sheepishly moved across to another peg.

Minutes later, another player strolled in and told me I was at his peg. So I moved again. The humiliating process continued until I eventually found a tiny area beneath the physio's bench, where I ended up keeping my stuff for the whole season.

My first league match for Bristol didn't start well either. When I walked up to the main entrance to the ground, feeling excited and pretty pleased with myself, the gate steward said he didn't have any idea who I was and refused to let me in. When I told him I was playing scrum-half for Bristol, he laughed. In desperation, I bought a match programme and showed him my name on the team list. He stared at me as though I was wasting his time.

Eventually Derek Eves, the club captain, arrived and asked the steward to let me pass, but he chuckled all the way to the team changing room and, while I was arranging my kit in the space under the physio's bench, the rest of the team had a good laugh at my expense. The student had been put in his place.

Recovering from these awkward beginnings, I settled quickly and soon grew to love everything about Bristol RFC. The supporters were knowledgeable and passionate, and most Bristolians appeared to be aware of the club and to know the players. Whenever we went out as a group, which was after most home matches, we would be admitted for free and welcomed with free drinks.

We were far from the most fashionable club in the country, but the team was a useful mix of youth and experience and, driven by unsung heroes like Derek Eves on the flank and centre Ralph Knibbs, we often surprised more glamorous sides. Even so, it was always a standing joke that nobody liked us, and that was why so very few Bristol players had been capped at international level. Happily, both that perception and the reality would soon change.

The pack of forwards deserved most of the credit for our rising profile. Guys like Mark Regan, Simon Shaw, Garath Archer and Alan Sharp were tough and competitive, and they made life seem a whole lot easier for the eager but still vulnerable youngster trying to make a name for himself behind them. I will never forget how, through that daunting first season of club rugby, playing against household names up and down the country, the Bristol forwards looked after me, protected me and helped me along.

Our biggest match of the season was the derby against Bath, who were then unbeaten and widely recognised as the top club in the country. I lined up against Richard Hill, the highly competitive former England scrum-half, who was apparently not too thrilled by a few press reports suggesting my recent form for Bristol could see me replace him in the No. 9 jersey of the South-West team.

Only a few minutes into the game I got caught in the middle of a maul and, as I managed to pop the ball back to my forwards, I felt two fingers plunge into my eyes. Any rugby player who has had his eyes gouged will understand what I mean when I say the pain was quite simply excruciating. I immediately let go of the ball and tried to wrestle these fingers away from eyes.

'Get off me,' I screamed in agony. I told the referee I had been gouged and, when he saw the redness around my eyes, he awarded us the penalty.

One of the other Bath forwards walked up to me and growled: 'This isn't student rugby any more, you *******
poof.' It was their No. 7 flanker, an excellent player, Andy Robinson, the selfsame 'Robbo' who would rise to fame as Clive Woodward's assistant coach. The Bath players tried to take cheap shots at me for the rest of the match. As the ball

bobbled out of one ruck, I scooped the ball up and sent an old-fashioned dive pass down the line. I thought it was quite effective, but Richard Hill obviously wasn't so impressed because he ended up running all over me.

Alan Sharp, happily forgetting how I had taken his peg, saw what happened and, believing it to be deliberate, went mad, raining punches on Hilly. It was an incredible response, and it took a referee, two touch judges and most of the players on either side to calm him down. Alan was a tough nut, and he had clearly decided nobody was going to bully his young scrum-half, accidentally or otherwise. I was grateful and, looking back, I wish 'Sharpy' could have been there throughout my career.

A little battered and bruised, I was still making progress and, at the end of the 1992–93 season, I was named in the England A squad to tour Canada. With most of the senior guys involved in the Lions tour to New Zealand, coach Geoff Cooke had taken the chance to blood some emerging players. I was obviously delighted by the news, together with my friends and family, but we soon realised the dates of the tour clashed with the final exams of my Law degree. I wanted to finish my course and I had always dreamed of playing for England, so there was a choice to be made.

The university authorities helped me out when, understanding my dilemma, they allowed me to sit my exams four weeks early, on my own, so that I could be available for the tour. Nobody had ever been given such special treatment before, to preserve the integrity of the exams, and I was sworn not to tell my mates what they would find when they sat the same papers a month later. Everything seemed OK, except for the fact that I was left with only three weeks to revise instead of seven. Just as I had before my A levels, I launched myself into my studies and, once again, I managed to emerge with a decent result.

It wasn't an easy time for anyone. Students facing their finals are a fragile breed, and I soon found myself being confronted by friends in floods of tears, begging me to say what was coming up in the exam, or imploring me to nod if they were revising the right subjects. I resisted temptation and kept my word. It was the least I could do for a university that had been good to me.

The A team tour to Canada went well: I started as a reserve but got a chance to play when Matt Dawson pulled his hamstring and I did OK. Just a few days after getting home, I was invited to join an England Under-21 tour to Australia, taking my place in a talented squad that included the likes of Mike Catt, Lawrence Dallaglio and Richard Hill, the Saracens flanker.

We won the Under-21 international, exactly a decade before another celebrated victory on Australian soil, and I managed to score a couple of tries, playing opposite a then unknown Australian No. 9 called George Gregan. Everything was happening so quickly for me, and everything seemed so easy. I was having fun training, having fun playing, learning, loving every minute.

Feeling the pressure?

I promise, it didn't even cross my mind. I was young then. Now, of course, pressure is something I'm much more used to, but I'm relaxed. Possibly the biggest match of my career is almost upon me, and I'm fine.

My hotel room is completely quiet now, and even the street outside is almost deserted. I'm lying in bed, staring at the ceiling, thinking about the game. It's strange. After all these years, after all the ups and downs, all the training sessions, after fifty-one matches for England, tomorrow could well be my last international.

I haven't said anything to anyone, but for some time I have been thinking that, if we do reach the World Cup final, there can be no better time and place to call it a day. So many sportsmen say they're going to go out at the top and never do it, but I have the opportunity and I'd be crazy not to take it.

Whether we win or lose, whether I get a run or not, that will be it, I think. I've had enough. I don't have the energy any more. I can't get myself going. There's nothing left. Right now, I'm sure tomorrow will be the end of the road for me. In about twenty-one hours' time, I will retire from international rugby. I think.

I've had a great innings. I can't complain. Everything seems to have flashed by when, in fact, it's almost ten years to the day since I made my England debut. I'll never forget that day. Nobody ever forgets the first time they play for their country.

It was a cold day at The Stoop, the Harlequins field across the road from Twickenham, and I clearly remember looking up to see Will Carling jogging towards me. It was the third week of November 1993, and the England captain was grinning. 'Well done, Kyran,' he said. 'Monkey is injured and you're starting.'

Oh ****, was my immediate reaction, I'm going to make my international debut against the All Blacks. Rumours had been doing the rounds all week that certain senior players were planning to withdraw from the New Zealand match on Saturday because they reckoned we would be trounced. I knew Dewi Morris, the first-choice scrum-half, was not one of them because I had seen how a chest infection had affected his breathing in training.

I was obviously thrilled, but the idea of playing the awesome All Blacks was daunting. They had already defeated the other Home Unions on tour and, although I had played in the South-West team that stretched them the previous weekend, most people seemed to reckon the tourists would trounce England.

'Don't worry, mate,' Will said, reading the expression of fear and apprehension that had spread across my face. 'Just do what you've been doing for Bristol, and you'll be fine.' Geoff Cooke came over soon afterwards and offered similar words of encouragement, but the coach wasn't looking too happy. He had lost an inspirational player in Dewi Morris, and had had to replace him with a rookie who had celebrated his twenty-second birthday two days before. If he's worried, I thought, how on earth should I be feeling?

With my head spinning as I tried to take everything in, an RFU official came over and told me that the rest of the squad would be returning to the hotel in the team bus, but that Jonathan Callard and I, as the two new caps for Saturday, would have to stay at The Stoop because the press wanted some photographs. I asked who would be looking after us. He smiled and said Jon and I would be fine, before strutting briskly towards the bus.

Never mind the All Blacks, ranks of the national media looked daunting enough to a young student, but we did as we were told, adopting all kinds of foolish poses. As soon as we got back to the hotel, we were taken into a press conference where, first up, Peter Jackson of the *Daily Mail* asked the question I dreaded: 'Why have you decided to play for England when, born in Dublin with Irish parents, you are better qualified to play for Ireland?'

'Well,' I replied carefully, 'I have lived in England since I was small, and played for England at Schools and Under-21 level, so I do have a strong sense of being English. Beyond that, I feel attached to the England rugby structures, and to the team-mates who I have played alongside moving through the ranks.'

I waited for a follow-up question from Peter, but there wasn't one. My answer seemed to be adequate, yet this issue of nationality would rumble through my career, especially in Ireland, where I have occasionally been taunted as some kind of traitor, both in bars and from the stands during matches at Lansdowne Road. To be frank, the matter has never bothered me. The facts are straightforward. I could have played for either country, but English rugby embraced me and gave me opportunities whereas, when I attended trials for the Irish Exiles in London, they told me, bluntly, that I wasn't good enough.

That's what happened, but there was no need to give all the details to the media on the eve of my first cap. They seemed happy and, after answering a few more questions, I was allowed to go to my room and begin making the phone calls I had been itching to make for the past four hours. My parents, my brother John and my sisters: everyone was delighted. A first cap is always a massive thrill for all concerned, and I was buzzing.

That cold Wednesday evening in November it was practically impossible to take the grin off my face as I wandered around the Petersham Hotel, Richmond. In such high spirits, I decided to play a practical joke on my room-mate, Graham Dawe, an experienced front-row forward, a true gentleman in every respect, and a Devon cattle farmer with hands like two bunches of bananas.

It was early evening when Graham wanted to borrow some shaving foam from another player, so he strolled along the corridor, wearing nothing but his underwear. Just then, I thought it would be funny if I locked him out of our room. So I did. He came back, found the door shut and calmly asked me to let him in. I suggested he go down to reception and ask for a new key.

He knocked again, a little more aggressively, then again much more aggressively. Before long, he was shouting expletives, telling me he would rip my head off unless I let him in. A crowd of players gathered outside our room, wondering what all the noise was about, and I started to wonder if the prank was quite so clever when Ben Clarke warned me to do as I was told.

'OK,' I said, by now a little nervously, 'I will open up so long as you promise not to lay a finger on me.'

'Fine,' he replied.

As I turned the key, Graham walked straight in and punched me in the face, knocking me to the floor. He then jumped on top of me and began mauling furiously at my face. The bunch of players at the door watched silently as the cocky youngster was given a hiding and taught to respect the senior players.

I had been an idiot, especially since I should have learned my lesson the previous Saturday when the squad assembled and I was told to room with Dean Richards, the No. 8. That afternoon, I had sprinted sixty metres to score the winning try for Bristol against Deano's club, Leicester, and he wasn't too pleased when he saw me sharing his room, so he skipped the team meeting and spent most of the night in the pub with Jason Leonard.

He still hadn't got back when I drifted off to sleep around

midnight, but I do know exactly when he did return because it was twenty past two in the morning when Deano and Jase stormed into the room, stripped back my bedding and lifted me up by my boxer shorts, giving me the wedgie to end all wedgies. My underwear was torn to shreds, and parts of my anatomy were cut.

After a sound pasting, I was told to get back into bed. Lying alongside Deano in that mood, I felt a bit like Goldilocks trying to fall asleep in a bed beside the big Daddy Bear. It was not a beautiful experience. There may not have been much I could have done to avoid that thrashing, except for not scoring a try against Leicester, but it should have taught me to recognise the importance of respecting senior players. If it had, I would have avoided the pounding by Dawe, my second big beating in four days. I hope it's not always like this, I groaned quietly.

On Saturday, 27 November 1993, I was woken at half past six in the morning by the gentle burble of the farming news on BBC Radio Four. Graham kept a small black radio beside his bed, which he used to keep up to date with the agricultural world while he was away with England. Being awake at this unearthly hour was not the norm for a happy-go-lucky, long-haired student from Bristol, but I had long since decided to keep my mouth shut.

We went down to breakfast together, where I scanned a few of the newspapers and saw my picture all over the place. A tabloid was branding me the Hugh Grant of England rugby, which I took as a compliment. As I sat there in the dining room, wolfing down toast and jam, everything began to seem surreal. Was this really me, the little tosser, the cocky student, in all these papers?

The morning before the international dragged, as I would

soon discover they always do, till we assembled for a team meeting at eleven o'clock. All of a sudden, I sensed the mood change within the squad. People who had seemed relaxed began to retreat into their own little worlds, each focusing on the challenge ahead, happy to be alone with their expectations, hopes and fears. As for me, I was too eager to be thinking about anything in particular.

Geoff Cooke spoke first, reminding us of the tactics: tackle them with everything we have; stop Tuigamala from playing; take points when possible, especially through Jon's boot; be brave and dig deep. Will then addressed his team, and he made a special point of wishing Jon Callard and me the best of luck. The speeches were followed by an emotive video showing England winning, and it ended unexpectedly with a clip of me playing for Bristol, making a break and scampering over to score a try.

I wasn't sure whether that shot had been put in the video to make me feel good, or maybe to reassure the rest of the guys that the new boy in the No. 9 jersey could do a job. Either way, watching it made the hairs stand on the back of my neck. Up till then I had thought that it was just an expression but, at that moment, it was nothing less than an accurate physical description. Right then, the realisation struck me hard right between the eyes: I was going to play for England.

When we boarded the team bus and headed for Twickenham, everyone was silent. Things go quiet before club matches, but there is usually total silence on the bus before an international. This was my first experience of travelling with a police escort, so I watched out of the window as the bus weaved its way through the match-day traffic. Everything seemed so new, so special. 'Just take it all in, mate,' whispered my roomie Graham Dawe, who was sitting next to me. 'You'll remember this day for ever.'

He wasn't wrong. As we arrived at Twickenham, everything that seems so familiar to me now was so exciting back in 1993. The bus passed the West Car Park, and I stared out at many thousands of people socialising near the boots of their cars, eating lunch and drinking champagne. St George's flags were billowing all over the place, and I was filled with a sense of being welcomed into something very strong, something weathered by passing decades, of being ushered into the fortress of English rugby.

We filed off the bus and headed to the changing room, with the cheers of the crowd standing around engulfing me. Now and then I could pick out a specific name being shouted, but there was an overwhelming din, a buzz of excitement more passionate and intense than anything I had known before.

The All Blacks arrived soon afterwards and, as I turned, I just caught a glimpse of big, stern men walking into the 'away' changing room. Tuigamala was huge, as alarming in his day as Jonah Lomu would be two years later, and Zinzan Brooke appeared so confident, assured and powerful, towering over his team-mates. I was just as star-struck by the legends getting ready beside me in our changing room: Brian Moore, Dean Richards, Will Carling, Rob Andrew and others. They had all been heroes for as long as I could remember and, today, I was wearing the same white jersey.

With a final word from Geoff Cooke and Will, we ran out into this vast bowl of noise and excitement. You want to let it wash over you, pass by like some huge wave in the sea, but the atmosphere swallows you up and scrambles your senses. You feel as though the 72,000 people in the stadium are looking straight at you, and you try not to imagine the millions watching on television, or even to think of your family and friends sitting up in the stand.

It's only another game, you tell yourself, just do what you have always done and relax, but, even as the words flash through your brain, you know very well that today they mean nothing. This is not a normal game. You're playing for England. Your reputation, your sense of self-worth, everything is going on the line. You might be a hero, or you might be a laughing stock. Everyone is watching, judging you. There is no escape. Deal with it.

The two national anthems seemed to go on for ever, but I got through 'God Save the Queen' with the rest of the lads and then followed Will towards the centre of the field, where we had decided to stand tall while the All Blacks performed the haka, the traditional Maori dance they do before every international.

I had thought about this situation before and, as the teams lined up opposite each other, I reckoned it could be a good idea to stare out my opponent, Stu Forster. However, when they started chanting and gesticulating, this plan failed because he refused to look anywhere near me and, somehow, I found myself positioned straight in front of Va'aiga Tuigamala himself.

Muscles bulging, eyes almost popping out, the man mountain was giving me the full works but, I thought to myself, I have seen that expression somewhere before ... ah yes, it was Graham Dawe in his underwear when I locked him out of our room. *Ka mate! Ka mate!* Just then, I wondered how the New Zealanders would react if we formed a circle and did 'Ring-a-ring-a-roses'.

Tuigamala was on turbo now, sticking his tongue out as if

he was going to eat me for dinner. That doesn't scare me at all, mate, I thought, mine is much bigger. I couldn't be sure back then, but I am reasonably certain now that I have the biggest tongue in world rugby. It may be a strange claim to fame but it's true and, looking back on that first haka, I wish I'd had the presence of mind to poke it out and wave it around for Tuigamala to see.

As the dance ended, I managed to catch Stu Forster's eye and I grinned at him, as if to say 'I'm going to sort you out, mate'. That made me feel great. I was excited and in awe but, as we prepared for kick-off, for the first time I also felt curiously comfortable. This was Twickenham; this was where I wanted to be.

Rob Andrew started the match; we won back the kick-off and began moving upfield. After a couple of phases, the ball appeared at the back of a ruck and I started to scamper around, intending to flick the ball out to Rob. As I moved, I felt a stud land heavily on my ankle, ripping open my sock. I shouted in agony. Jamie Joseph, the All Black flanker, had caught me. I was the new boy, and he had formally welcomed me to world rugby.

I couldn't move. My first thought was that my England career was over almost before it had begun. I lay still on the grass and told 'Smurf', our team physio, what had happened. He knew what he was doing and reckoned a bit of strapping would do the job. Get up, I told myself, don't go off. Just hobble around and pass the ball, if necessary, but make sure you finish the match.

Somehow, I managed to get through the game, concentrating on the basics, not trying to do much on my own. I made a serious mistake early in the second half, when the All Black full-back ran past me, but Victor Ubogu covered for me and bundled him into touch. Following the tactics, we were tackling for our lives, keeping Tuigamala quiet on the wing and Jon Callard was kicking the points.

Against every prediction, England won 15–9, beating probably the best team in the world at the time. Everyone was ecstatic, and I seemed to become a focal point of the celebrations. Apparently, the Joseph stamping was clear on the television replay, and I was cast as the plucky newcomer who had suffered a preconceived assault, got up off the floor and helped secure a great win. I could tell from the reaction of my team-mates things had gone well for me.

The mood in our changing room was electric, and I remember looking across to see Will Carling smiling broadly, lying back in one of the famous old baths reserved for senior players and swigging from a bottle of champagne. He beckoned me over to get into an empty bath beside him, which one of the experienced guys had just left, and I did as I was told. Will then passed me the champagne, told me I'd had a great game and ordered me to take a gulp.

Could life get any better than this? Here I was, having helped defeat the All Blacks on my debut, soaking up the pleasure in the England changing room at Twickenham, reclining in one of the baths alongside legends like Carling, Moore and Andrew, passing round bottles of champagne, laughing, feeling great, in fact feeling about as happy as it was possible to be.

The day became a joyful blur. My ankle had swollen up like a balloon, so I was using crutches when I was called forward in the home changing room to receive my first England cap from HRH Prince Edward. Then, at the post-match reception, even the New Zealanders were being kind. Their captain, Sean Fitzpatrick, said in his speech I had played like a seasoned All Black, which, coming from him, was probably the biggest compliment of all.

It's an England tradition that new caps have to sing a song on the team bus while we travel from the stadium to the post-match reception. Jon Callard and I decided to sing our own duet version of 'Close Your Eyes' by Bebel Gilberto, and we were both subjected to the usual torrent of abuse by the rest of the squad.

Another custom was that, in the course of the evening after your first international, every other player in the team buys you a drink and skulls one with you. Mercifully, Terry Crystal, the England team doctor, saw I was on crutches and, as I downed a tenth glass of wine, told the senior players to go easy on me, thus sparing me the fate suffered by Austin Healey a few years later. After his Test debut, Aussie was forced to drink so much that the consequent vomiting ruptured a blood vessel in his eye and he took weeks to recover from the alcohol poisoning.

I was pleased to be in a reasonably sane state later that night because Geoff Cooke came and sat beside me. He said I had played well, but suggested I should study a video of the game to see where I could improve. He was calm and knowledgeable and, although I worked with him for only a few months, it was clear to me, and most players, that he was ahead of his time. In many respects, Geoff was a professional coach in the last days of the amateur era. He was always extremely well prepared, in planning our training and tactics as well as in analysing opponents, and his gesture of including my try for Bristol in the video before the All Black game was the kind of smart, perceptive thing that Clive Woodward would do a decade later.

The players appreciated Geoff because he was a great

believer in continuity and keeping the same team together. This worked insofar as the guys got to know each other really well, but the downside was that some senior players were put in a comfort zone where, no matter how they played, they stayed in the team. People like Moore and Carling sometimes seemed untouchable. Clive's decision to put Lawrence Dallaglio on the bench for his fiftieth cap proved that kind of preferential treatment doesn't exist today.

However, Geoff set the standards in his era and, through six successful years as England coach, from 1988 to 1994, highlighted by Grand Slams in 1991 and 1992, and an appearance in the 1991 World Cup final, Geoff carefully established strong structures around the team upon which our future glory would be built. His teams tended to rely on the domination of a big, powerful pack, the leadership of Will Carling and the kicking nous of Rob Andrew. Cleverly making the most of the talents of Dick Best as his assistant, Geoff guided England out of the dark ages to a stage where they became a real force in world rugby. I was a big fan, and would have liked the opportunity to play for him more often than I did.

On the Monday morning following the win over New Zealand, my chances of keeping my place in Geoff Cooke's side were dented when a scan on my injured ankle revealed a partial dislocation and a few bits of bone floating around the joint. The doctor said I would be out of action for three months, and added that it could only have been adrenaline that had got me through the match.

Rugby history is decorated by stories of people playing through horrendous injuries, none more amazing than the tale of how the All Black Wayne Shelford completed a Test, only to discover afterwards in the changing-room showers that one of his testicles had almost fallen out of his scrotum. My dislocated ankle pales by comparison, but I was quietly proud to have finished the game.

Even today, people frequently ask how my ankle is feeling, but I rarely tell them the truth, which is that it feels very weak, and subsequent knocks haven't helped, and that I take care to strap the joint before every training session and every match, just to ensure it doesn't turn and rip the ligaments. I can't complain. Persistent injuries are a fact of life for almost all rugby players.

As for Jamie Joseph, he was apparently handed an internal punishment by the tour management, but there was no public sanction, and he was in and out of the All Black Test side for the next two seasons. He then signed a contract to play in Japan, for whom he went on to play at the 1999 World Cup. Oddly, I later played a club match against him and made a special point of treading, not too hard, on his ankle. Sadly, this was not a notably successful act of revenge, because I succeeded only in damaging the ligaments in my own ankle, while he got up and jogged away.

Three months on the injured list opened more time for me to enjoy the celebrity status that seemed to have been bestowed upon me in the aftermath of my debut. I didn't really have any idea what I was doing, but just wanted to appreciate it all because I didn't know how long the front-page photographs, the personality profiles in glossy magazines, the feature interviews and even the appearances on morning TV were going to last.

I was quickly signed up as a client of Park Associates, who also acted as agents for Will Carling, and some fools started talking about me as a future England captain. I had played one Test. After a while, I began to feel embarrassed by the fuss and attention, and started to worry that people would look at me and think I was an arrogant little sod. I really wanted to be humble.

After completing my degree, I had moved on to law school in Bristol, and my classmates thought it was a great laugh that their fellow student was suddenly being followed by television cameras and getting attention wherever he went.

Some of my mates even took it upon themselves to answer the mail that began to arrive in the letterbox, typically from teenage girls wanting an autograph or a date. They thought it was hilarious to write back, pretending to be me, proposing a time and place to meet. My girlfriend at the time didn't reckon it was quite so funny, but nothing went too far. Everything was fun. The future seemed to stretch out before me. I couldn't wait ...

That seems such a long time ago. Glancing at my watch, I see time is hurrying on towards half past one in the morning. A quick graze through the channels proves there's nothing on television, so I reach for an old edition of the *Sydney Telegraph*, which is lying on the floor beside my bed, and start to read.

I'm feeling tired, ready for a decent sleep. Hopefully, I'll drift off to sleep while I'm reading the paper.

Not quite. The *Sydney Telegraph* is hilarious. I laughed out loud the first time I saw that story, and it's worth reading again.

'Grumpy Old Men: Has England's ageing pack ambled past its use-by date?' and 'Ancient Art of Bore: It's the English national pastime' are a couple of the headlines. Some clown called Mike Gibson has written an article picking up on the general Aussie theme that our team is boring, old and predictable. If there was a time when England rugby teams were upset by this kind of baiting, it has long passed. Nowadays, we think it's hilarious.

Under the caption 'Suddenly, nothing interesting happened . . .', the newspaper has printed six photographs, of Nick Faldo, Steve 'Interesting' Davis, Captain Valium Geoff Boycott, Tim Henman and Hugh 'Tedious Twit' Grant. 'We're talking about a nation of people whose idea of excitement is to join a queue,' he writes.

In fact, the guys at the *Sydney Telegraph* are a laugh. One of their reporters came to our hotel wearing a 'Stop Jonny' T-shirt, and they have even constructed a sign on the beach near our hotel that reads: 'Danger! Boring Rugby Team Trains Here'. The players enjoy this kind of messing around as much as anyone. Maybe we are able to take such a relaxed view of the constant attacks because this England squad prepares to play the Wallabies knowing and believing we can win. We don't fear them at all, and we don't feel inferior to them in any respect.

This hasn't always been the case. When I first started playing for England, international rugby seemed to be played in two leagues with the three southern-hemisphere giants – New Zealand, Australia and South Africa – on top, and the four Home Unions, France and the others struggling along behind. We did manage to beat one of the big guns once in a while but, by and large, especially away from home, we were overwhelmed by opponents who were bigger, faster and stronger. So the extent of England's realistic ambition was to win the Five Nations, and maybe a Grand Slam. We had a different perspective.

In 2003, an England victory in Paris, Edinburgh, Cardiff

or Dublin might be regarded as nothing more than expected but, nine years ago, such results were viewed as huge achievements, reasons to celebrate.

At the start of 1994, the powers of the south could look after themselves, in their own world. I wanted nothing more than to be part of an England team that played well and dominated what was then the Five Nations Championship.

The general expectation was that I would retain my place at scrum-half, ahead of Dewi Morris. Pundits were saying I had a better pass than the more experienced No. 9, and that this would allow the back line more space and time. That was overstated, but I was the media's 'flavour of the month' and having such a great time I was stupidly starting to believe my own publicity.

In truth, as I know now, the level of my skills was nowhere near high enough for international rugby, and I could never match Dewi for knowledge and experience. Maybe he should have been selected for England's opening match of the 1994 Five Nations, against the Scots in Edinburgh; perhaps I was trading on the glory of my debut against the All Blacks and got the nod. In any event, I wasn't short on self-confidence, or even cockiness, and I carried that attitude onto the field at Murrayfield.

Gary Armstrong was playing scrum-half for Scotland, as ever a bustling and inspirational presence behind their pack, but some people felt he had a weakness passing off his left hand. I thought it would be a good idea to remind him of this, so early in the game I stood on his foot and challenged him into showing everyone that he didn't have such a crap pass off his left hand. I remember he was a bit shocked that I had spoken to him like that.

In any case, a few minutes later Gary put the ball in at the next scrum, collected the ball at the base and sprinted away down the blind side, crossing our line in the corner. The try was disallowed for a double movement, but the Scot had made his point and he wasted no time in coming up to me and saying: 'Who needs a pass when I can do things like that, you little ****?'

Scotland might have been trounced by the All Blacks, who we had then beaten, but in this game they matched us in every phase and, trailing by two points with very little time left, we were really lucky to get a late penalty. The referee said he had seen a Scottish hand touch the ball in a ruck, but the television replay later proved it was one of our players who had handled the ball.

To a chorus of boos around the ground, Jon Callard stepped up and kicked the fifty-metre penalty that gave us a 15–14 win. The final whistle sounded soon afterwards, and we sprinted back to the changing room, grinning like cats who'd stolen the cream. We knew we hadn't played well but, against the old enemies at Murrayfield, we were very happy to take any kind of victory.

Will strolled off to the post-match press conference, and the captain came back twenty minutes later with an even broader smile on his face, bursting to tell us what had happened. Apparently, he had arrived for a television interview and been asked to wait until Gavin Hastings, the Scottish captain, was finished.

However, Gavin was so upset by the result that he was struggling to get through his answers without breaking down and, every time this happened, the television producer stopped the tape and said they would have to start again. Will was waiting patiently, and he thought it would finally be his turn when Gavin seemed to compose himself and approach the end of his ordeal.

Then the interviewer asked Gavin to watch the monitor and offer his comment on the clip that clearly showed an English player handling the ball on the ground before the decisive last penalty. That was a mistake, because it prompted more tears. Then, mercilessly, they showed him how Jon Callard had moved the ball forward a couple of yards from where the penalty was awarded, and pointed out that his kick had only just cleared the crossbar. By this stage, Gavin could scarcely speak. Admired as one of the most honest and emotional guys in the game, he found losing to the old enemy hard at the best of times, but it seemed intolerable to be denied a rare victory over England in this way.

Will recounted this saga with tears of mirth in his own eyes, and everybody was soon roaring with laughter. Each of us respected Gavin hugely, but it was hard not to see the funny side, and we were still smiling when we left the ground and slipped away to the bars of Rose Street to celebrate our good fortune.

My honeymoon period in the England set-up ended abruptly nine days later when the squad gathered in Richmond ahead of our next Five Nations match, against Ireland at Twickenham. The press had been critical of our performance against Scotland and, at our first session, the forwards and the backs were divided to talk about what had gone wrong for us at Murrayfield. The consensus among the three-quarters was that we had kicked away too much ball and never threatened to break through out wide.

That seemed reasonable, but when we got back together with the pack I was told how, in the forwards' discussion, I had been blamed for not varying the line-outs, making it easy for the Scots to predict our moves. Well, it *was* my job to call the line-outs but, if I was getting it wrong, I wondered why some of the more experienced forwards, such as Brian Moore, who was approaching his fiftieth cap, hadn't said anything to the emerging scrum-half playing only his second international match.

I was hurt. Everyone had been so kind to me and everything had been going so well that the first hint of criticism, the first sign of the politics that runs like an undercurrent through every sporting team, was a shock. All of a sudden, I wasn't smiling. I began to feel a bit insecure and vulnerable. International rugby, I was learning, is not a breezy picnic where everybody loves each other. It's a jungle, and you have to be tough and thick-skinned to survive.

We were under pressure to win, and the last team you want to be playing in that situation is Ireland. They're a ferocious bunch who feed on scraps of possession. When you play against the Irish, the senior guys told me, you feel like you're playing against thirty men, not fifteen. They come at you from everywhere.

My Irish roots predictably became an issue for the media in the build-up to the game, which didn't bother me, and I even had a laugh with some of my cousins from Skerries when they said they didn't know which side to support. However, I was taken aback when, getting warmed up in our changing room at Twickenham, I overheard some of the Irish players shouting at each other that they wanted to 'get the traitor Bracken'.

The words stuck in my mind. Were they simply using me to psych themselves up before a big game? Or did they really think that? The exact phrase seemed to stay with me. In nights to come, it would crop up in some of my worst dreams.

I started the match feeling like a marked man, and focused on getting my pass away as briskly as possible but, after about half an hour, the ball looped towards me from the top of a line-out. It seemed to hang in the air for ever and when I took the ball I also took the full force of the Irish pack. They ran all over me, shoeing the living daylights out of my body. Worse than that, as I picked myself up off the ground, the Irish won possession from the ruck, stormed upfield and scored a try in the corner.

The Twickenham crowd, which had celebrated so noisily when we beat the All Blacks, seemed stunned. Trudging to our posts for the conversion, I realised my shorts had been ripped to shreds and called to the bench for a new pair. As I did so, a couple of Irish lads walked right past me and, grinning, said: 'There's plenty more where that came from.' They were right, and I ended up taking a physical battering for the rest of the match.

There was, however, a moment of minor consolation for me when, late in the game, the Irish lock Paddy Johns tried to whack me at the base of a ruck. I saw the punch coming, dodged out of the way and watched as Paddy's nose was broken by one of his team-mates, who was trying to hit me from the other side. That story may sound too Irish to be true, but Paddy confirmed it years later when he became my team-mate at Saracens.

We ended up losing 13–12. I had had a poor game, missing a few tackles, taking a few dodgy options. Perhaps those comments earlier in the week had undermined my self-confidence and belief; maybe the open Irish antagonism had unsettled me and got into my head; more likely, I just wasn't as good as everybody – most of all me – had so quickly started to believe.

Hero against the All Blacks, zero against Ireland: this was my reality, and I was struggling to accept the disappointment when, early on the following Monday morning, I saw that the *Sun* had included me among six England players who it showed with their heads on the block, ready for the chop from the selectors. So soon after being praised, I was being criticised. I fell hard, from a 'future England captain' to a 'former England scrum-half' in a few weeks. The *Sun*'s information turned out to be good and, sure enough, when the squad reassembled I did get the dreaded knock on the door from Geoff Cooke.

Over the past decade, I have become something of an expert on being dropped by England coaches and, amid my frustration, it has been quite interesting to observe how they have gone about the task. Geoff used to wield the axe most gently. Whenever possible, he would call on your room, knock on the door and ask for a quiet word. The guys cottoned on to this and, on the night before the team was going to be announced, players under threat often used to hide in other rooms, hoping the coach would battle to track them down and change his mind in the meantime.

Well, unfortunately, Geoff had no trouble finding me, but he was sympathetic, quietly telling me Dewi was back in the team for his experience, and that I shouldn't worry because he was certain I had a bright future. Even so, I was gutted. If winning my first cap had been the ultimate high, then getting dropped for the first time was the ultimate low. I suddenly felt ashamed, as though I had let everybody down, especially my family and friends.

Now, in those days, anyone who had been dropped generally had to pack up their stuff and go one of three ways: either straight home, or two hundred yards up the hill to join the B team at another hotel, or to a room with another guy on the bench. Playing in a specialist position, I was invariably dropped to the subs, which meant I stayed in the squad. That happened this time, and I was shifted to share a room with the reserve fly-half, Stuart Barnes.

He was in a foul mood because he had just been told that, yet again, he was on the bench behind Rob Andrew, even though Rob hadn't had a great game against Ireland. Barnsey hadn't taken the news too well. In fact, he'd had a real go at the coach, telling him he was never going to drop 'his golden boy'. By the time he got back to what was now our room, he needed to calm down, so he called the bar and ordered an expensive bottle of red wine for himself and a few bottles of Grolsch for me, the student. 'That can all go on the RFU account, thank you,' he said, before putting down the phone.

I was feeling pretty disappointed myself, but I had to spend the next couple of hours lying on my bed, listening to the trials and tribulations of being Stuart Barnes, aged 31½. Nearing the end of a long career, when ten England caps didn't seem to reflect his natural ability, he complained about spineless management and favourites in the team. Although I didn't know it at the time, I was getting a sneak preview of Barnsey as an acerbic pundit. Within a few months, he would start his second career, as a resident rugby commentator and expert at Sky Sports television.

That night, he brooded way past midnight and then started to read a volume of poetry, which he had been asked to review for *The Times*. He only turned off his light at three in the morning and even then I couldn't get any sleep because he started to snore like no other room-mate I have known, before or since.

I remained on the bench for the rest of the 1994 Five Nations campaign, which was followed by Geoff Cooke's resignation and the appointment of Jack Rowell as the new England coach. Dewi kept his place for the tour to South Africa but, out of the blue, Jack put me in the team to play Canada at home in December, and I had one of my best games for England in a 60–19 win, rounding off a move that started inside our own half to score my first international try.

Back in favour, I took a conscious decision to keep everything in perspective, stay calm and, most important of all, to work even harder on improving my skills. I reckoned I had always been a committed trainer, but I thought I would have to take my game to a higher level to keep my place in the England side.

Richard Hill was widely reckoned to be the best passer in the game, so I plucked up the courage to call the guy who had once trod on me in a Bath–Bristol game and ask his advice. When he might easily have told me what to do with myself, Hilly went out of his way to help, breaking down my passing technique and then giving me one-on-one training once a week for several months.

I began to improve and, when Hilly said he usually practised by doing 200 passes off each hand four times a week, I told myself I would make 201 passes off each hand six times a week. I wanted to have the best pass in England and became gripped by the goal, even to the point of taking a rugby ball with me whenever I went on holiday so I could keep up my routine. When I read how Daley Thompson was so eager to get ahead of his rivals that he trained on Christmas Day because he knew others would be resting, I decided if it was good enough for the Olympic decathlon champion then it was good enough for me, and trained on 25 December.

Nothing was too much trouble. I wanted to pay the price.

So I trained, and trained, and trained. Dad joined my cause, often standing beside me while I practised my passing, waving a big stick above my head to make sure I stayed low, and then kicking at my hands to make sure there was no backswing. My fingers and knuckles were sometimes cut and bruised by the time we finished, and training often seemed more dangerous than playing a match, but it was worth it because I wanted to improve.

The hard work paid off, and Jack kept me in the team for our first match of the 1995 Five Nations, against Ireland in Dublin. We won 20–8, and then beat France 31–10 at Twickenham a fortnight later. I was playing well in a successful side and, for the first time, started to feel as though I really belonged.

Spirits were high when we assembled in Richmond to prepare for the fixture against Wales in Cardiff, and most of the players decided to get on the hose, having a few drinks in a local pub, the Sun, and then moving on to the Park Avenue nightclub. I must have drunk seven or eight pints of beer, in a vain attempt to keep pace with Jason Leonard, and at about three in the morning Mike Catt and I decided it was getting past our bedtime.

We arrived at the hotel and used the back stairs to get to our rooms but, hearing noise in the team room, I wanted to see what was going on. Alcohol was clouding my judgement and, to my horror, I opened the door to find Jack and Les Cusworth, his assistant, still up, watching a Wales game on video. Les turned and saw me, but I got away before Jack looked around. At least, I think I did. I couldn't be sure. This was bad. If Les told Jack who he had seen, they could possibly throw me out of the squad and send me home. I managed to get some sleep, but woke the next morning with a hangover. When I heard the coach had called a meeting, I prepared for the worst.

Quite a few of the guys weren't looking too bright as we took our seats in the team room, and I certainly got the impression that the whole place stank of alcohol. Everybody seemed to be in a bit of a haze when Jack stood and started to speak.

'One member of the side came in at 3 a.m. last night, pissed out of his head,' the coach said, standing tall. 'With an important game on Saturday, that's a disgrace. Les knows who it was, but he is not prepared to tell me, so I've decided to leave this whole issue for the captain to investigate and resolve.'

That was that. Then, as the management team filed out of the room, all trying to look as stern as Jack, Jason Leonard whispered to the players: 'Well, it weren't me, 'cos I only got back at half past five this morning.' Everyone fell about laughing, but Will Carling wasn't too happy and, when I admitted to being the one who Les had seen and it emerged that Mike Catt had been with me, he said he would deal with the pair of us later.

We travelled to Cardiff the following day and, that evening, Mike and I were called to Will's room. I tried to explain it was all my fault because I had peered into the team room, but I also couldn't resist noting the irony that, in actual fact, Catty and I had been just about the first to get back to the hotel.

Will wasn't too bothered by our version of events, and he laid into us, calling us a couple of immature kids with fewer England caps than fingers on one hand. We tried to look sorry and dejected when he said we were getting above our station, but it was hard not to laugh with the rest of the guys when we told them what had happened. All we had learned was Rule One: don't get caught.

Of course we had behaved badly but, in my experience, such incidents never do much harm to team spirit. On the contrary, they often show a squad is happy and confident, and we duly went on to beat Wales 23–9 in Cardiff. It was a great game, and it was followed by a great night out, courtesy of Victor Ubogu.

'The champagne's on me,' our genial prop declared in the changing room after the game. Victor always fancied himself as a bit of an entrepreneur and he told us how, before the match, he had noticed the bookies offering odds of 10–1 against him scoring the first try of the game. He thought he would have a bit of that, so he asked a friend to place a bet of £100.

Sure enough, he proceeded to score the first try and he was so pleased with himself afterwards that he couldn't resist telling everybody, including the reporters, how he had backed himself and won a thousand pounds. The RFU officials weren't so happy with him, because players putting bets on themselves raised all sorts of match-rigging issues, and they warned him not to do it again. Since then, following some scandals in football and cricket, it has become illegal for any player to bet on a match they're playing in.

In any event, Victor hosted the squad to a night on the town in Cardiff, but the story didn't end there, because when he called to collect his winnings, his mate told him he was very sorry but he hadn't thought there was any chance of a prop scoring the first try, so he'd used the stake to buy himself a match ticket. We all thought that was very funny but Victor, for once, fell quiet.

Three wins out of three took us into a Grand Slam/Triple Crown/Championship decider against Scotland, who had also won their first three games. Twickenham was packed, and we proved too powerful, winning 24–12 in front of our own supporters.

'Swing Low, Sweet Chariot' echoed around the stadium and, amid all the celebrations and excitement, we were swiftly installed as favourites to win the 1995 Rugby World Cup, starting in South Africa eight weeks later. Jack was hailed as a coaching genius and each of the players was praised to the skies. Some of the guys were flying high, lapping up the headlines and soaking up the plaudits, but many of us were more cautious. Of course we were delighted to win a Grand Slam, because they don't come around that often, but, in truth, we hadn't played particularly well in the Five Nations and, deep down, we knew we would have to produce a lot more to become world champions.

Well, according to the media, if anyone could guide England to the ultimate prize in the game, it was Jack Rowell, the man who had coached the team to glory in his very first season. However, as players, we tended to have a more critical eye.

Tall and upright, Jack had earned a reputation as a successful businessman, working for several companies, and, back in the amateur era, when most players worked during the day and trained only in the evenings, he had been able to combine his business career with 'coaching' the hugely successful Bath team, although it did seem he had been more of a manager than a coach.

Leaving most of the technical work at Bath's training to senior players like John Hall, Andy Robinson, Richard Hill and Stuart Barnes, who effectively ran the sessions, Jack was content to focus on his own particular brand of motivation. This method was based on a belief that players would respond to censure, so he sometimes goaded them by being cutting and critical, by making jokes at their expense, by prodding and probing them to perform.

It seemed to work. Bath continued to dominate the domestic game and, when the RFU needed a successor to Geoff Cooke, they looked no further than big Jack. Naturally, he brought the same bag of tricks that had been successful at club level, but it wasn't long before they caused rumblings in the national squad. On one occasion, when Alex King, the young Wasps fly-half, was invited to train with the England squad for the first time, and everyone was gathered in the changing room, Jack turned to the nervous youngster and said: 'Ah, how are you?'

'Fine, thank you, Jack,' Alex replied.

'No,' the coach said, 'I said "who are you" not "how are you".'

Well, he got his laugh, and Alex blushed, but I wondered what benefit Jack saw in embarrassing a young lad like that. That was just his way. When most players, even at the highest level of the game, need to be supported and built up, Jack sometimes preferred to needle them. His first words to me after putting me in the team to play Canada the previous December had not been 'well done' or 'good luck' or anything like that: he said he 'couldn't believe he had picked a Bristolian'. Of course, he was only joking, but that kind of remark doesn't do much to build confidence.

Then, the morning after that particular game when I had played so well, I walked straight out of the hotel lift and faced an area where Jack was having a meeting with his coaches. Just as I tried to tiptoe past, unnoticed, the coach called out: 'Bracken, you should stop trying to run down blind alleys!'

What? What had he meant by that? Everybody laughed, and I smiled awkwardly as I hurried on, but I didn't have a clue what he was talking about. It subsequently emerged that Jack had only been trying to say he thought I was playing too much on my own, which was probably fair comment, but why hadn't he just come out and said that instead of trying to crack another joke? Players prefer coaches to be blunt and straight, not to talk in tongues.

Jack wasn't going to change. At one particular team meeting before the match in Cardiff, he had made a point of asking Graham Rowntree how we were going to beat Wales. Then, before the prop could answer, the coach interrupted and said: 'That'll be all.' Again, he got a laugh. Again, he would say he was joking, but just what was the good of making Graham feel stupid?

Inevitably, as Jack poked fun and ridiculed us, the players began to poke fun and ridicule him. At another team gathering, he was using an overhead projector when a fly landed on the projector, creating a silhouette on the screen. The coach saw this, but tried to brush the fly away from the screen. Some of us started to snigger, because the fly was obviously on the projector, and we couldn't help but laugh out loud when the coach began looking behind the screen, waving his arms at the silhouette. Even the fly, still sitting quite happily where it had always been, on the projector, must have laughed.

Even so, notwithstanding the misgivings over his motivational style, Jack Rowell deserved credit for gathering together an England squad that balanced youth with experience and, at the very least, seemed ready to challenge at the

1995 World Cup. Unfortunately, his and our preparations for the tournament were disrupted by the uproar that blew up when Will Carling cracked a joke of his own, describing the RFU Committee as '57 old farts'.

Every player agreed with him, of course. We had all grown to resent the entire blazered old-tie brigade who continued to run the game, blissfully removed from reality, living in a time warp, trying to cling to their free tickets and preferential parking passes, and a golden amateur age that had long passed. How could we think anything else when, under huge pressure to perform in a modern era of media and television scrutiny, we had to stand by and watch farcical events such as our highly respected kicking coach being chased off the training field because his very presence was a breach of the amateur code?

It would have been funny if it weren't so pathetic. Dave Alred was renowned worldwide as a kicking coach, and we were delighted when Jack hired him to work with us. However, one day when we were about to start training at Twickenham, Dave was approached by Don Rutherford, our own Technical Director at the RFU, and told he was not allowed to stand on the same field as us because he was a professional, having been paid to work in the US National Football League and also to play rugby league in England, and his presence could seriously jeopardise our amateur status.

We couldn't believe it, but then Don said he thought it would be fine for Dave to continue coaching us from the sidelines, because then he wouldn't technically be on the same field. It was difficult to blame Don, a decent guy who had to defend the indefensible, but when we were all working hard to compete against the southern-hemisphere nations, it was mind-boggling that our efforts should be regularly undermined by such petty nonsense.

Before long, the Australians heard what had happened and invited Dave to help out the Wallabies. How could we think anything other than that the game was being run by '57 old farts'? Will's only crime was to state the bleeding obvious, but the captain was promptly sacked for making the remark and, a few days before we were due to fly off to the World Cup, England rugby was plunged into a crisis of its own making.

RFU officials started discreetly asking senior players whether they would be prepared to lead the side to South Africa but, to their eternal credit, without exception, each of the guys refused and said they wanted Will to captain the team. Such solidarity forced the Union to backtrack and, having persuaded Will to apologise to the Committee, they reinstated him as captain.

Bonded as never before by this saga, the players travelled to the World Cup with real optimism, but the tournament unfolded as an ultimate disappointment ... both for the team, because we collided with a remarkable player called Jonah Lomu, and for me personally, because events somehow didn't seem to go my way.

As we arrived in Durban, where we were scheduled to play our pool matches, all anybody seemed to be talking about was the issue of altitude. Four of the match venues were at sea level and the other four were at around 5,000 feet, and everyone had their own opinion on what needed to be done, in each different scenario, to minimise the effects on the players.

Most of us weren't too bothered because Durban is by the Indian Ocean and the schedule meant our potential quarter-final and semi-final would be at sea level as well, in Cape Town, but our management was fixated by altitude, and they provided each of us with a special diving suit that was designed to make us sweat like pigs, raise our core body temperatures and therefore reduce the debilitating effects of altitude if and when we advanced to play the final at Ellis Park in Johannesburg. In fact, the suits made us look like stark raving lunatics, and we hardly wore them.

However, we all had altitude on the brain and it was not long after arriving in Durban that the squad went for a jog on the beach, and Victor Ubogu is reputed to have turned to one of the guys and said: 'Wow! This altitude is a real killer.' As an Oxford graduate, he insists he never said anything of the sort, but it always gets a laugh when a speaker uses it at a function. Unfortunately for Victor, some stories just become enshrined in rugby folklore.

I was nursing a sore back, not for the first time nor the last, so Dewi Morris was given a start in our opening match against Argentina, but I was recalled for our victory over Italy, played well, and appeared to have regained the No. 1 spot that had been mine since the previous December. The coaching staff then took me aside and told me I would be rested for our last pool match, against Western Samoa, but assured me I had been pencilled in to play in the quarter-final.

That seemed OK, but nothing is ever certain in rugby. I got on to play the last five minutes against Samoa, not at scrum-half but as a flanker, because Rob Andrew and I were the only substitutes left when Dean Richards got injured late in the game. Rob was quick enough to hide from Jack's view, so I was sent on and immediately got run over by their big No. 8. Meanwhile, Dewi had played an absolute stormer, looking strong and sharp, and made himself impossible to drop ahead of the quarter-final.

So I was back on the bench, once again buying sweets for the rest of the subs because I was the youngest reserve. Sometimes it happens like that. It wasn't my fault; it wasn't even Jack's fault. I was playing really well, but so was Dewi, and he was named in the team to play Australia, the defending champions, in Cape Town. Much to my delight, the guys produced a big performance on a big day, and Rob Andrew won the game with a late drop goal.

It was one southern-hemisphere power down, with two to go, because we faced New Zealand in the semi-final, with probably South Africa to come in the final. Life wasn't getting any easier, but we were running into form and, as Jack said, we had defeated the All Blacks only eighteen months before; although nobody needed to be reminded that that was before the arrival of Jonah Lomu.

The giant left wing had emerged as the star of the World Cup, appearing unstoppable as the New Zealanders swept all opposition before them. He was quicker than our quickest guy and stronger than our strongest guy. It wasn't fair but, amazingly, through all our team preparations before the semi-final, we never discussed a special plan to stop Jonah.

Hindsight is always the perfect science but, even at the time, many of us were astonished when Jack told us Tony Underwood, our swift but diminutive right wing, would mark Lomu as usual and that he had 'no worries about that match-up'. He shot off a couple of smart one-liners, and everyone was laughing when we should have been creating a strategy to stop Jonah: we could have aimed to stop him before he built up any momentum and, once he was flying, we could have planned to double-tackle him, with one guy going low and the other taking him at chest level.

Instead, we did nothing and Lomu literally ran all over us, scoring four tries and winning the semi-final on his own. Tony did his best, but nobody could have stopped Jonah on their own, and he did get some compensation when the two of them later starred in a Pizza Hut advertisement based on their contest.

We crashed out of the tournament, and suddenly something that could have been so great seemed so flat. When all the players wanted to do was to fly home, we had to play a pointless third-place match against France and then wait another four days to attend an official Rugby World Cup dinner after the final.

South Africa won the Webb Ellis Cup, playing with guts and successfully bringing Lomu down to earth. Most of us reckoned the tournament had been set up neatly for them, and they had been lucky to beat France in a waterlogged semi-final that could easily have been abandoned, but sitting in the stadium it was impossible not to be moved by the sight of Nelson Mandela in his Springbok No. 6 jersey and the spectacle of the new democratic South Africa uniting in support of the rugby team led by Francois Pienaar.

The home win apparently sparked a series of fantastic parties across the country but, unfortunately, we had tickets to the worst of them and the official dinner was a shambles. The Springboks turned up hours late and Louis Luyt, the SARFU president, made an awful speech that was supposed to be funny but just sounded arrogant. Most of us were openly heckling and jeering by the end.

When we were eventually allowed to fly home, I began to feel very disappointed not to have had more opportunity to contribute to the campaign. Dewi had done well, but I had started the tour as the first-choice scrum-half, played in one full match and played well, but somehow found myself back on the bench. Jack hadn't said a word to me, so I went to discuss the situation with Will.

He said he thought it may have been because my pass was not as sharp as Dewi's, which shocked me, but at least he was honest. When I raised that issue with the coaching staff, they mumbled something about me lacking experience. Conflicting messages left me confused and frustrated. All any player wants to know in that kind of situation is precisely where he stands.

I was actually recalled for our last match of the year, at home to South Africa at Twickenham, but I didn't have a great game and we were well beaten by the new world champions. To be honest, I shouldn't even have played because I was suffering from a serious bout of glandular fever but, when you get the chance to represent your country, it's difficult to say no. You ought to say no, of course, because, having worked so hard to get there, it makes absolutely no sense to jeopardise your reputation when you're not 100 per cent. That is the logic, but it's not always so easy to apply.

We were due to play Western Samoa a month later but, ready for bad news, on the day when the team was due to be selected I was doing a photographic shoot for Simpsons with Ben Clarke, the England flanker. It was turning into quite an embarrassing exercise because the photographer made me stand on three London phone directories to get somewhere near Ben's height.

My mobile telephone rang while I was balanced on this perch, and I knew I had been dropped, yet again, as soon as I saw Jack Rowell's name appear on the LCD display. He was decent, saying he wanted to give Matt Dawson a run, telling me not to worry, urging me to hang in there and get back in the frame.

A few minutes later, my mobile rang for a second time and, once again, I saw Jack's name appear. I answered the call, and Jack's first words were 'Hello, Victor'. I couldn't resist laughing, and telling him that meant Victor Ubogu was dropped as well. Jack was embarrassed to have got his numbers mixed up, but I was right.

Matt held his place, and I remained on the bench throughout the 1996 Five Nations, when a narrow defeat against France in Paris cost us another Championship. However, I did get on as a substitute against Italy at Twickenham in November, and so kept my record of playing for England every year since my debut.

Injury ruled me out of the 1997 Five Nations Championship, when the guys again finished runners-up after another three-point defeat to France, this time at Twickenham, but I recovered in time for the Lions tour to South Africa and was very disappointed to miss out on selection for the initial tour party. Instead, I was included in a substrength England squad, without our Lions, named to tour Argentina during May and June 1997.

Jack Rowell was coming under increasing pressure and, aside from one last Test against Australia, this was to prove his swansong as England coach, but he continued to provide several moments of 'Classic Jack', which the players really enjoyed.

The coach's dilemma was that so many of the players on the tour to Argentina were newcomers, and he seemed to have great difficulty in remembering everyone's names. He kept calling Danny Grewcock, our lock forward, Dan Arnold, who was actually the team administrator. When he just didn't know a name, he referred to the player by their club and position; so, most of the time, Jim Mallinder was known simply as 'the Sale full-back'. These problems came to a head at a meeting called to name the side for the first Test against the Pumas. Jack had taken care to write the names down on a piece of paper but, unfortunately, he'd then left the list in his room. Now, he was on his own.

As the players sat in silent anticipation, Jack got through the front row all right, named the locks without a problem, but came to a grinding halt at the back row. He paused for a moment, turned to ask Les Cusworth, his assistant, who was playing back row. Les said he didn't know. Jack paused again, then asked Mike Slemen, the backs coach, who they had selected in the back row. Mike couldn't remember either. As players, sitting open-mouthed in amazement, we really didn't know whether to laugh or cry.

For some of those players, being named in that England rugby team was meant to be the crowning moment of their career. For the rest of us, it was nothing less than embarrassing. We managed to draw the series against the Pumas, but Jack's days as the England coach were numbered. The RFU didn't treat him well towards the end, keeping him hanging on while they were obviously searching for his successor, but he eventually resigned with dignity and credit after more than three years in charge.

The edition of the *Sydney Telegraph* is still lying open on my bed, and I chuckle to think how Jack Rowell would have responded to all the Pom-bashing about being boring. He would certainly have fired back a few jokes of his own, but the big difference between then and now is that, then, we didn't have the confidence to really take on the Australians and ram this kind of thing right back down their throats. Now, things are different. It feels like we're on another level, and we expect to win every match we play, whether it's against the Boks, Blacks or the Wallabies – anyone. That's how far we've come as an incredibly well-prepared, dedicated professional international team under the guidance of Clive Woodward.

Anyway, it's almost two in the morning and the World Cup final is going to kick off in just over eighteen hours. I wish myself a Happy Birthday, turn over and finally get back to sleep.

CHAPTER THREE

7.18 a.m.
Saturday, 22 November 2003
ENGLAND TEAM HOTEL, SYDNEY

Opening my eyes, I am relieved to see early-morning light creeping between the curtains of my hotel room because it means I've had a decent night's sleep. The last thing I wanted was to wake up and find everything still dark. The start of the World Cup final is just thirteen hours away, but that seems a long time to wait. I wish it was an afternoon kick-off instead of a night match.

I draw back the curtains and am amazed to see three hundred of our supporters already hanging around in the street outside the front of our hotel. Most of them have travelled halfway around the world just to be here, and they seem drawn to this place, hoping for a glimpse of someone, or even an autograph. Somebody is pointing up at me, so I immediately step back from the window because I don't want to be spotted, don't want to hear my name being chanted, don't want to draw attention to myself. Now into my eleventh season as a member of the England rugby squad, I suppose I'm not so excited by the limelight and the adulation as I once was.

I don't think I've ever been on the A-list, provoking the kind of hysteria that Jonny, Johnno and Clive get, but I am sometimes aware of people looking twice when they see me in the street, and I do get recognised by people who follow rugby. The vast majority of the population walk on by, though, which suits me.

It was different when I was young. I was so excited to see my picture in all the newspapers on the Monday after my debut against the All Blacks, so pleased when we were let into nightclubs for free and given drinks on the house, so flattered when people called me the new 'pin-up boy' of English rugby, so proud when I appeared as a guest on *The Big Breakfast*, the cult show on Channel Four, and presenter Gaby Roslin kept squeezing my leg.

Life was fun. My mobile never stopped ringing, I was getting a stream of invitations to do this and that and, for a while, I seemed to have been touched by the magic wand of celebrity. Naturally, I lapped it up, accepted whenever possible, scribbled autographs for anyone who asked, grinned, laughed, joked and loved every minute of it. Any twenty-two-year-old would have done the same.

Agents flattered, and I listened. They told me I had a cheerful and clean-cut image that came over well on television, so I agreed to be a guest presenter on *Rugby Special* and started to appear on regional programmes in the southwest. That went OK and, after a while, producer Andi Peters asked me to be a presenter on *Train 2 Win*, a kind of junior *Gladiators*, on ITV.

On my first day, I panicked when they told me to go out and warm up a live audience of 4,000 hyped-up kids and their parents, but Andi and my co-host, Margherita Taylor, coached me along and within a few minutes I was whooping it up, getting one side of the arena to make more noise than the other. This was completely new territory, but I relaxed and enjoyed the experience, even when I had to interview children who offered only one-word answers, even when I fluffed my lines on 'take nine' and even when the audience laughed at me because I'd dropped the medals I was supposed to give the contestants.

The opportunities continued to flow and I was invited to be a guest on *Through the Keyhole*, the show where Loyd Grossman presented a film of inside your flat or house and then a studio panel asked questions before trying to guess your identity. Unfortunately, I was away on the day the camera crew wanted to film my flat, so I arranged for my mate, Grant Bulstrode, to be there and make sure everything was looking neat and respectable.

Grant took the opportunity to plant a card in the living room with the words 'Thank you for a lovely night. Love always, Grant.' It was the kind of prank that sounds funny in concept, but turns out to be a nightmare in practice. Anyway, the studio panel studied the film, but didn't guess it was my flat; then I had to walk on and spend the interview trying to explain Grant's sense of humour.

Television propelled my name and face beyond rugby, and the number of letters I received rose to ten or fifteen a day. Most were sent by teenage girls wanting a signed photo, which I was happy to provide, several were more suggestive and just a few were from blokes. One day I got a letter asking me to write 'With Love to . . .' and then the name of a pub, which I can't remember, on an enclosed photo. I did exactly that and, a year or so later, Jason Leonard said he had seen a signed photo of me in a gay pub in London. Jase thought that was hilarious, although he never properly explained why he had been there in the first place.

Now, the England supporters are just milling around in the street outside our hotel, some reading newspapers, some chatting, a few of them are even into their first beer of the day. As I stand here watching, I feel really appreciative towards them. Young and old, guys and girls, student back-packers and rugby fanatics, they have all paid enormous sums of money to be here, and the players appreciate them as an important part of our cause.

That's the least we can do, because they effectively pay our salaries through the tickets they buy and the merchandise they wear. People talk about the money in the game as if it comes from the sponsors or television companies; in fact, it passes through those companies when the punters buy their satellite subscriptions, mobile phones or whatever. At the end of the day, everything starts with the fans, those people standing in the street. I've tried to keep this in mind through-out my career, and if that means spending a few more minutes signing autographs after the game when you really want to go home, or even having a chat with a stranger in a hotel foyer, then so be it.

That said, through ten years spent in varying degrees of the limelight, my attitude towards the public has changed. It hasn't all been a 'laugh' or just 'a bit of fun'. In fact, there have been several occasions when the attention has left me feeling uneasy, uncomfortable, used and extremely vulnerable.

An invitation to do a photo shoot for *Cosmopolitan* looked harmless enough. I might be only 5' 10" tall, but I had done some modelling for Simpsons, the menswear store, so I was quite relaxed when I turned up at the studio and met the photographer. He then introduced me to a make-up artist, who was rubbing her hands in oil. This struck me as strange, so I thought I had better ask her what clothes I would be wearing for the shoot.

'Nothing, of course,' she replied, adding she had been asked to rub that shiny lubricant all over my body.

No way. There was just no way in the world I was going to take my kit off, and I told her so. Nobody had warned me this was the deal, so I phoned the agent who had booked me, but she said she knew nothing about it. Something didn't make sense. I was under pressure. People in the studio told me the shots would be fine, but I couldn't stop thinking about what my mum would say.

The stand-off continued for a couple of hours, until I said I would do the shoot in my boxer shorts. They agreed, but a loincloth was suddenly produced and wrapped around my waist, and within moments the photographer was snapping away. Feeling awkward and more than a little angry, I just wanted him to finish so I could get out of the place and forget about the whole thing.

That turned out to be easier said than done. 'England rugby player bares all for *Cosmo*,' yelled the headline in the *Daily Express* a couple of weeks later. I was mortified to see the photos, which had been cunningly taken to make it look as though I was wearing nothing except the skimpy loincloth. My family and friends were initially surprised but ultimately more sympathetic when I explained exactly how the shoot had happened.

It became clear that *Cosmopolitan* had asked a hundred well-known people to strip for the camera, and only four had agreed: an actor from *Casualty*, somebody off *Baywatch*, the presenter of *Eurotrash* and me. I was criticised by a few rugby officials and feminists and, needless to say, my team-mates were merciless.

Everything seemed to have blown over a couple of weeks later when I went into hospital to have my tonsils removed. I was watching television in the room when the nurse arrived to check my blood pressure ahead of the operation. At precisely that moment, my *Cosmo* photos suddenly appeared on the screen. They were the topic of discussion on *This Morning*, and I had to sit there, blushing almost as much as the nurse, while Richard and Judy debated the pros and cons of my controversial decision.

Looking back, I suppose this kind of notoriety could possibly be part of the reason that I began to attract the kind of attention that makes you feel scared rather than special, that makes you feel vulnerable rather than admired. From the autumn of 1995 into 1996, I learned what it means to have a stalker.

It all began when Simon Shaw and I went for a couple of drinks at a nightclub after an England training session. We had a good time and met a couple of girls, who gave us a lift home, nothing more. One of these girls then appeared at my flat the next day. She said she was just returning my credit card that, she insisted, I had left behind at the club. That was strange, because it's well known that I'm usually very careful with the contents of my wallet. In any event, her visit did not thrill my girlfriend at the time and, despite my protestations of innocence, our five-year relationship ended.

Single again, I started going out more regularly, but noticed this girl always seemed to be around. Whenever I went for a drink, she appeared in the same bar, offering me a drink. Even when I came out of the changing room after playing for Bristol, she was often standing there, mingling in the crowd. Of course, I can look back now and see something was seriously wrong but, at the time, I was naive enough to believe these apparently accidental meetings were nothing more than a series of coincidences.

After a few weeks of this, she approached me and asked if we could be more than friends. I said no, and thought that would be the end of the matter. It wasn't. She started dating a series of my mates and somehow stayed in my social circle. At around the same time, I started to get a series of strange telephone calls where the person on the line said nothing, breathed heavily for a minute or so and then hung up. I know I was being stupid, but I reckoned it was just some of my friends messing around.

The penny finally dropped when, around midnight at the same nightclub where we had first met, she begged me to give her a lift back to her place. I refused and left for home. Just forty minutes later she was on my doorstep, knocking on the front door, clearly distressed, her top torn, claiming she had just been attacked by four lads who had jumped out of a red Ford Capri.

Nothing really added up from the start, but I opened the door and said we should immediately call the police. The constable came, took her statement and, even though I expressed my reservations to him, he insisted I let her stay the night. It was hardly ideal, but I asked her to sleep on the sofa and retreated to my bedroom, locking the door behind me. She predictably came knocking, but I pretended to be asleep and survived till morning.

The entire situation was getting to me, so I arranged to see a lawyer friend and, following his advice, approached the detective who had been assigned to the case. I told him everything and said I thought she might have faked the whole attack so that she would have an excuse to spend the night at my place. He replied that he was already thinking along similar lines.

The police eventually got hold of her phone records, saw she had made at least sixty calls to my number over the previous month and charged her with wasting police time. She insisted she was innocent of everything and the case fizzled out but, at last, she left me alone.

Maybe this kind of hassle goes with the territory and anyone with a public profile simply has to accept that, every now and then, they are going to attract trouble. All you can do is be careful, stay calm and roll with the punches, sometimes literally.

Some time ago, I was minding my own business at a club in Bristol when a girl came up to me and started talking about rugby. Five minutes later, this guy punched me from behind and wanted to know why I was chatting up his wife. Before I could say anything, six guys laid into me and I was getting kicked from all sides, until the bouncers came to my rescue and pulled me away.

Simon Shaw was out with me that night, but he had been in the toilet during the fracas. I told him what had happened and he wanted to go back and take them all on, but we persuaded him that was not a good idea. The manager asked if I wanted to call the police and press charges, but there was no point. Headlines such as 'England Player in Nightclub Brawl' were not going to do me any good. As the saying goes, if you fight with pigs, you get dirty, but I took a cab home that night, knowing there was nothing I could have done to avoid the incident.

More recently, I have been subjected to a far more invidious kind of attack. Cuts and bruises quickly heal and are soon forgotten, but hate mail lingers and plays on your mind. One day, when I was going through the pile of letters kept for me at the Saracens office, I could hardly believe what I read: 'Next time you play for England, make sure you sing the national anthem, you Papist Irish ******* piece of ****. You don't deserve to wear the rose, you Paddy *******. We're watching you.'

My first response was to laugh it off. Anyone who could write a letter as abusive and pathetic as that was unlikely to be someone worth worrying about, but then I began to wonder whether I should start singing the anthem, just to be safe. What did they mean when they said they're watching me? Did they know where I was living? Were they cranks, or were they serious?

I eventually showed the letters to the police, who said they had a pretty good idea of the kind of person who would write that kind of letter. They managed to collect some fingerprints from the letter, but nothing matched in their records.

Anyway, I'm definitely going to sing the national anthem at the stadium in Sydney tonight. Sometimes I don't sing because my mind is so focused on what I will have to do in the match, but tonight is different: England against Australia, the 2003 World Cup final, one chance. There'll be time to concentrate on the game after the anthem.

François Pienaar once told me he had decided not to sing the South African anthem before the 1995 World Cup final because he thought he would burst into tears. Well, I can understand exactly what he meant but, tonight, in tune with all those supporters still standing in the street outside, I'm going to sing my heart out.

*

It's unusual for a modern professional rugby team, but the guys have hardly mentioned money for a few weeks now. In many ways, even for the players, this Rugby World Cup is about glory and getting the job done for a country that hasn't celebrated victory in a major team sports event since 1966.

However, this game is also our living, and I would happily bet my match fee that there isn't a member of the squad who isn't fully aware that, if we do win tonight, each of us will get something like £70,000 for the whole World Cup campaign. That might not seem much to footballers like Thierry Henry and David Beckham, who are supposed to earn that amount in a week, but it's a lot of money to us humble rugby folk; and, moreover, we all know what battles we had to win and how we had to struggle to get where we are today.

Rugby union was the last of the major team sports to turn professional at the highest level, so it was surely not unreasonable to expect that the transition from an amateur code to an open, paid sport would be relatively uncomplicated. After all, the same issues had been resolved and the same structures created in other sports.

In fact, calm reform was too much to expect. Several weeks after the 1995 Rugby World Cup, the International Rugby Board suddenly announced the end of amateurism and declared the game open, prompting six years of trauma, bitterness and infighting in English rugby. The three main parties – the RFU, the club owners and the players – seemed constantly in dispute, and I found myself involved in this saga, initially because I was working as a trainee solicitor at the time and some players relied on me to understand the complex negotiations, and latterly when I served three years as a board member of the PRA, our players' association.

The old amateur code had been ignored to varying degrees in different countries. Leading South African players had been paid for years, and everyone knew the stories about boot money in Wales, but, to a large extent, very little cash changed hands in England. A club used to attract a player by helping him find a lucrative job, and I had been introduced to my law firm by a rugby contact, but, even as late as 1994, I was still playing annual subs to Bristol RFC as my contribution towards the running of the club.

In August 1995, the floodgates swung open. The RFU tried to retain some control by freezing the frame, announcing a one-year moratorium on professional rugby in England, but a succession of wealthy businessmen started emerging to invest in the clubs – Nigel Wray began to transform Saracens, Sir John Hall lured Rob Andrew to overhaul Newcastle, Tom Walkinshaw took control at Gloucester – and the players were having their heads turned by a plan to stage an unofficial global rugby circus, something like the Kerry Packer series in cricket eighteen years before.

A representative of TWRC (The World Rugby Championship) arranged to see me and David Powell, a senior partner at the law firm where I worked in Bristol. He outlined their plans and asked us to help them sign the top sixty rugby players in England on contracts that looked amazing: superstars like Will Carling and Rob Andrew would get £250,000 per year, internationals like me would be paid £135,000 per year and players outside the England squad would be offered annual salaries of around £80,000.

There seemed no harm in exploring the option, so we agreed to assist TWRC and began arranging a series of cloak-and-dagger meetings up and down the country, signing up the players without the RFU or the media knowing what was happening. I didn't know if the project would get off the ground, but it was exciting. After so many years of filling stadiums and getting nothing, we were being offered what seemed unbelievable salaries.

Before long, David and I had stored sixty signed contracts in the safe deposit box at our offices in Bristol. Identical documents were being signed by top players in all the major rugby-playing countries and, for a while, it seemed as if everyone was united, from the French to the New Zealanders, from us to the Wallabies, prepared to overlook the more onerous provisions, like the one saying any player could be forced to play anywhere in the world, and eager to see if the TWRC adventure could get off the ground.

It didn't, because the Springboks accepted their Union's offer to match the terms and ripped up their provisional agreements with TWRC. Without the 'world champions', the 'world championship' was never going to work. Many players blamed the South Africans for letting everyone else down, but they had simply played their cards cleverly, and each of them ended up with an enormous, essentially unconditional three-year contract. In any case, I am not convinced TWRC would ever have worked, because it relied too heavily on a new format of regional rugby, when it is only the international game that has ever generated substantial revenue.

TWRC was gone, but it had become clear that, as top English players, we were going to be offered decent salaries as professional sportsmen. The issue was now how this money, flooding into the game from sponsors and television rights, would be channelled to the players: would we sign contracts with the RFU, who would then lend us out to the clubs, or would we contract directly to our clubs, who would

claim subsidies from the RFU? This dilemma caused the conflict within English rugby in the late 1990s.

More players' meetings were held, and the consensus
leaned towards signing with the clubs, who were offering
real money, rather than the RFU, who were still barking out
threats about banning us from playing for England. Everyone was adamant that we should all stay united and avoid
being picked off one by one but, inevitably, divisions began
to emerge, most notably when Will Carling came out in
favour of remaining loyal to the RFU and against signing
with the clubs.

Many of us felt disappointed. The entire squad had
backed him to the hilt when he was fired as captain before
the World Cup, and made sure he was reinstated, but now,
when it was essentially our futures on the line, he didn't seem
to be supporting us. This sentiment erupted at one meeting
when, as Will started to put the RFU case, one of the players
turned on him and said: 'Shut the **** up, you scab. We
don't know why you're here anyway.'

Everyone burst out laughing, and Will just sat there,
blushing, isolated. The players eventually opted to sign with
the clubs, and each of the sixty who had signed with TWRC
received an inducement payment of £30,000, paid by
EPRUC, the clubs' organisation, in two instalments. We
might not have hit the jackpot, but it seemed a reasonable
outcome.

Towards the end of 1995, getting used to life as a professional rugby player with Bristol but still not cashing the
salary because of the RFU moratorium, I decided to resign as
a trainee solicitor with Alsters in Bristol and focus full-time
on rugby. Part of me hesitated to stop before completing my
qualification, especially because David Powell, a good

friend, and the other partners had been so generous in allowing me time to pursue my rugby, but the demands of training and pursuing a career were too great.

I was waking up at six in the morning, throwing a couple of hundred passes, then doing a full day's work at Alsters, trying to do my bit in the office, and then training with Bristol in the evening. It was too much. Something had to give and it certainly wasn't going to be rugby, so I drifted away from a legal career.

Our decision to sign with the clubs had effectively created a basic structure for professional rugby, but the point of conflict then became the sum of money the RFU would pay the clubs. The Union was banking the game's primary source of income – sponsorship and television rights relating to the England squad – yet the clubs were paying the main item of expenditure, players' salaries.

I believe the transition would have been easier if the RFU had directly contracted the top sixty players right from the start, following a model successfully deployed in New Zealand, but what was done was done, and we had to exist in our own landscape.

The clubs and the Union fought over money incessantly and, through the crises and ultimatums, as players we inevitably tended to side with the club owners who were signing our cheques at the end of each month. This situation fomented distrust between the England players and the RFU, and it was hardly surprising when the tension exploded into open conflict in 2000.

Our complaint was straightforward: the Union had signed a massive multi-million pound rights deal with Sky Television, plus they had the international match ticket income, and they were using our image rights ... and yet they were still paying us a match fee of £3,000 plus another £2,000 if we won. When we raised the issue, they responded by cutting our ticket allocations for international matches at Twickenham. Each player had been used to receiving three tickets for free with an option to buy an additional ten; now we were told to expect three for free and an option to buy seven.

Nothing upsets an international rugby player quite as much as messing with his tickets, especially when that player happens to be a Catholic scrum-half with a large family to satisfy. The guys were absolutely furious, and we sent representatives to start negotiations with the RFU. These dragged on for months, with no progress, until our people came back and said the only way we were going to get anywhere was by threatening to strike.

Our initial response was negative. As a group, we wanted to keep on playing for England – that was all any of us had wanted ever since we were boys – but we would be pushed only so far. With the autumn internationals imminent, we asked our representatives to go back and try again. Still nothing. We beat Australia before a full house at Twickenham the following Saturday and hoped the success would persuade the Union to be more cooperative. The RFU officials couldn't even find time to schedule a meeting.

We were fast running out of options. Argentina were our next opponents at Twickenham a week later, and some people suggested doing what the Premiership footballers had done and making our protest by staying in the changing room for ten minutes at the start of the match. That idea was dismissed because it would upset the television people, and we had no gripe with them.

The S-word was starting to loom large. When we were

meant to be preparing for the Pumas, we were quietly gathering to talk about a strike. Johnno took the lead, pointing out that the RFU's attitude was forcing us to take action. Whatever we did, whether we opted to strike or not, he said, we had to do something. He didn't want to push us one way or the other, but he reckoned the squad needed to discuss every option and make up its mind.

I had sat through many England team meetings, but never one quite like this. The atmosphere was electric. Everyone listened intently to each word that was said, and it soon became clear there was a range of opinion. Some of the younger guys just didn't want to rock the boat, while the old hands like me had had enough of being short-changed and rebuffed by the Union. The talking carried on until Neil Back proposed we take a vote. 'Whatever the majority decides, either yes or no, we all go with it, OK?'

Everyone agreed. Each of us was given a piece of paper and told to write either 'yes' or 'no' to going on strike before Saturday's match against Argentina. As I made my vote, I thought there could not be many more traditionally conservative groups of people in England than the national rugby team, but the RFU had effectively forced us into industrial action.

The vote was overwhelmingly in favour of a strike, although I know of at least two players who voted 'no', one of whom was my good friend, Richard Hill. I asked him why, and he explained he just didn't want anything to get between him and playing for England, not money, not tickets, nothing. I understood his view and told him so. There were no hard feelings. 'Anyway,' Hilly said, 'I'll go along with the majority decision, as we agreed.'

Our three representatives, Martin Johnson, Matt Dawson

and Lawrence Dallaglio, were then given the task of inform-
ing Clive and the management of our decision. He reacted by
immediately calling yet another team meeting, which began
with the players shuffling into the room, trying to avoid
catching the coach's eye. Each of us was looking down at the
ground, while team officials stood around looking angry. I
felt as if I was back at school.

'I can't believe you guys,' Clive began, his eyes popping. I'd
thought he would be angry, but not this angry. 'You're going
to get slaughtered in the press if you go on strike. I don't want
to work with a group of players who take this action.'

Johnno responded. When his players were under attack,
even from our own coach, he was never to be found wanting.
'So, you're resigning, Clive? Is that what you're saying?'

'No,' replied the coach, slightly taken aback. 'I said I'm
not prepared to work with this bunch of guys again.'

'Oh, I see,' Johnno said. 'So you're going to withdraw
your labour. You're basically going on strike as well.'

Clive was fuming by now, telling us we would be regarded
as mercenaries by our supporters and saying we were
making a huge mistake. Andy Robinson added a few stern
words of his own, and some of the players didn't know
where to look.

Johnno was not backing down, and he stopped the
meeting by reaffirming that the players had made their decision and suggesting to Clive that he talk to Francis Baron,
the RFU CEO, and persuade him to discuss some kind of
compromise. Many players left that meeting believing their
England careers were over. Nobody was joking. This was
getting serious, and each of us knew it.

The coach wasn't giving up either. He was proved right
about the media when the newspapers reacted to the news by

branding us stupid and greedy, and he began telephoning the players, one by one, asking them to reconsider their decision. Some of the younger guys were looking like nervous wrecks after taking Clive's call, but we stuck together and Johnno calmed them down.

On the second day of the 'strike', the Wednesday night, the squad attended a fundraising dinner for Alastair Hignell at the Café Royal, and we arrived to find photographers and TV crews everywhere, eager to get pictures of the 'rebel rugby players'. We all took care to avoid Clive, which was probably just as well because he didn't look as though he wanted to talk to us either.

There seemed no sign of a solution, and yet, within twelve hours, Peter Wheeler, Fran Cotton and Clive had met with Francis Baron, and we had got a deal. We had said we didn't want win bonuses when we played for England, because money was not going to make us try any harder, so our match fee was raised to a straight £5,000 per match, which was fine, and bonuses were set for winning a Grand Slam, summer tour, an autumn series or a World Cup. Our image rights were going to be shared and our match-ticket allocation reverted to what it was before.

None of this was going to bankrupt the RFU and, despite the amazing vitriol hurled at us in the newspapers, no fair-minded person would have begrudged us remuneration that put the annual earnings of a regular England player, in a winning side, at no more than £45,000 on top of his club contract. In the end, I was left feeling it had all been quite petty, but money was never really the issue for us. We had set out to establish a principle that the England players should always be heard, not ignored like errant children. That much had been achieved.

Peace broke out, and Clive looked as relieved as anyone. At a meeting the next day, he told us that he stood by what he said but that it was all water under the bridge. 'By the way,' he added, smiling again, 'when I call for a chat, don't call me "Babs".'

Mark Regan had an odd habit of calling people 'Babs' instead of 'mate', and it seemed that, when Clive phoned him to discuss the strike, he had kept calling the coach 'Babs', which hadn't gone down too well. The players laughed. It was good to hear that sound once again, and we hoped the trials of the previous few days would prove to have made us an even stronger, tighter squad.

Relations between the RFU and the players have been calm ever since the strike, but that incident did not resolve the problems between the Union and the clubs, and the rows over the allocation of RFU income created hostility that spilled into other issues such as annual relegation from the Premiership. The Union saw the one-up, one-down plan as a crucial incentive for clubs in the lower leagues, while the clubs saw it as an unnecessary and perhaps catastrophic trap door that jeopardised their vast investment.

The club owners, who were essentially bankrolling the league out of their own pockets, became progressively disenchanted and eventually called a meeting with the PRA board, including me, where they told us they were unable to keep paying 350 players in the Premiership without support from the RFU. They wanted every player in the league to sign a declaration that they would not play for England until the matter was resolved.

'In fact,' said Tom Walkinshaw, chairman of Gloucester, 'we want those signatures within twenty-four hours, or the party's over and we'll have no choice but to stop paying the players.'

We staggered out of the meeting, struggling to come to terms with yet another crisis, yet another ultimatum. Eventually, we went back with our own list of demands: fewer matches each season to prevent burn-out, a larger percentage of the league's television rights income to fund the PRA and a seat on the EPRUC board. The clubs agreed, and we began chasing signatures.

Players' meetings were urgently arranged around the country and, again, there was some reluctance to threaten a strike, but the club owners also attended and when they made it clear to their own employees that they would stop paying them unless they signed the declaration, nobody really had much choice.

The RFU was told, and was outraged, initially threatening to expel the entire Premiership from the Union, but the usual bluster was eventually followed by a deal. It was agreed one third of the Union's income would be distributed to the clubs, equivalent to an annual grant of £1.8 million to each club. At long last, seven years after the sport had turned professional, English rugby had finally created a viable structure, accepted by each of the three major stakeholders in the game: the RFU, the clubs and the players.

I had become a bit concerned that my visible role in the midst of all these developments would put a black mark against my name at the RFU, jeopardising my England career. There was no question of me standing back, because I believed in what we were doing, but I also didn't want anyone at the Union to think 'Bracken is more trouble than he's worth'. In fact, there was no reason to worry. To their credit, the Union bore no grudges at all.

Looking back over this period, professionalism has

obviously changed the game beyond recognition. I played at the highest level as an amateur, when we trained in the evenings, and then also as a professional, when we sometimes train all day, and I can see how this evolution has brought significant benefits. Even the most ardent former player would agree standards have been raised: players are generally well paid and free to focus on being the best they can be; investment has transformed most of the clubs and league attendances have steadily increased; and the England team is the best prepared in the world. The game has also become more important. What used to be the fun part of the players' lives, something we did because we loved it, has become our living.

Imagine a guy who goes out for a drink with his mates now and then. He enjoys it and has a great time. Then, one day, a businessman turns up and offers him a decent salary to go out for a drink every morning, every afternoon and every night. It sounds perfect, so he accepts. As time passes, he still enjoys going out, because he likes his drink, but the experience somehow starts to feel different. It has suddenly become more 'important' because it's now his living. An element of fun has been lost.

In some respects, this has been my experience as an amateur rugby player who went professional. I am not complaining, because I am being paid very well to do what I love doing, but I am also not blind to the unfortunate fact that rugby union often seems to have stopped smiling. It's become a tough business.

Back in the amateur era, at club and international level, it was normal practice for the two teams to eat together and have a beer, or three, after the match. In fact, we often used to go out and stay over, spending the Saturday night at an opponent's house. I recall many drunken nights with Mike Catt in Bath.

This kind of thing doesn't happen any more, partly because the game has become so 'important' that, almost by definition, any losing team must go into mourning, and be seen to do so. Anybody having a drink after a defeat would risk being accused of not taking the game seriously, or not being committed.

I am also afraid professionalism has subtly changed the public perception of rugby players. It felt good to be seen as a blameless amateur, building a sound career and scoring tries for England in our spare time. People generally seemed to like us, and our various excesses were tolerated with a good-natured grin.

That often seems to have changed now. I sense members of the public look at us and see just another group of highly paid professional sportsmen, chasing the next cheque as hard as they chase their opponents. The old tolerance has gone as well. Where once we got the benefit of the doubt because we were unpaid, now we are employees, disciplined and ruled in terms of the contract we have signed, the contract that feeds our families.

Anyway, that's life. Money isn't everything. True, if we do win the World Cup tonight, we'll all get a £15,000 bonus, and that will be welcome. However, some time ago, I watched a programme on television where Sam Bartram, the Charlton Athletic goalkeeper, was looking back on his life. As he sat there, he was holding his 1947 FA Cup winner's medal and he looked at the camera and said so long as he had that, he would never be poor.

If we can beat Australia tonight, irrespective of match fees and win bonuses, we'll never be poor either.

＊

Finals are different because one single individual error can be the difference between triumph and defeat, between sensing you've had a fantastic career and feeling ultimately unfulfilled. It's like putting a huge bet on the outcome: you win big, or lose big.

I've had this feeling before, when Saracens were preparing to play Wasps in the 1998 Tetley's Bitter Cup final. It wasn't the World Cup final, and the worldwide television audience was a fraction of what we'll have tonight, but it was a colossal day for everyone at Sarries because we had never won anything before.

That match was the culmination of a period when Saracens were widely admired as the model club of the professional era. A long-time supporter named Nigel Wray, who also happened to be a property millionaire, effectively transformed a low-key team playing its home matches in a north London park into a dynamic, brilliantly marketed team drawing crowds of up to 20,000.

Nigel's investment was initially used to bring four established international players to Bramley Road: Philippe Sella, the legendary French centre, Michael Lynagh, the great Wallaby fly-half, Francois Pienaar, the world champion Springbok, and me.

The decision to leave Bristol before the start of the 1996–97 season was one of the most difficult of my career. I enjoyed living in the city, had a good relationship with the supporters, really loved the club and always intended to remain there. However, an untidy series of events combined to leave me thinking there was no option but to make a fresh start somewhere else.

One day in December 1995, a couple of Bristol officials

heard I was preparing a statement to the media and, at a time when Rob Andrew had been recruited by Newcastle, jumped to the conclusion I was about to move. The Board hastily gathered and offered me a deal worth £100,000 per year to stay at Bristol. In actual fact, the press release I had been preparing was to announce my resignation from the law firm, but now this fantastic offer was on the table. I accepted, and was happy to have resolved my future.

In the weeks that followed, my lawyer and I tried to complete what we thought would be the formality of getting the deal signed on paper, but nothing happened and Bristol seemed to be regretting their offer. There was still a verbal contract, but we couldn't enforce it because there was a moratorium on professionalism. As the situation dragged on, I became really frustrated.

My patience snapped when, with no progress on my contract, and me still playing as an amateur, I learned the club had already been paying other players, Arwel Thomas and Derek Eves. We were near the bottom of the league but, with fourteen matches to go, I said I would not play unless they honoured their commitment. They responded by paying 25 per cent of the deal, and I agreed to carry on playing, hoping things would eventually sort themselves out.

Our season ended, and Bristol announced that contracts would be offered to players on three tiers. As an international, I was told I would be put on the top tier. Everything seemed fine, and I was just about to sign on the dotted line when I phoned Garath Archer to see what he had been offered: the figure he told me was more than I was getting. Once bitten, twice shy, I was not going to be taken for another ride and, within a week, I was sitting in the restaurant at a service station on the M4 motorway, signing to play for Saracens.

The media automatically assumed I had moved for money, but this was not true. In fact, the contract that I left unsigned at Bristol was worth slightly more than the package offered by Saracens. My move was prompted by the breakdown in my relationship with the Bristol officials, but this transition was a difficult period for everyone involved in the game and I bear no grudges. Far from it, I hope Bristol RFC win every game, except against us.

So I prepared to start the first professional season of English rugby at a brand-new club. Saracens was buzzing, like a fine old car that had just been fitted with a V12 engine. Anything was possible, and these were exciting times to be involved.

Oddly, the game had entered a twilight world where we knew we were professional, because the cheques began to arrive at the end of each month, but nobody seemed quite sure how to behave in the new order. We were feeling our way. For example, my first idea was that I would continue to live in Bristol, where my friends were, and would drive to London for training and matches, a four-and-a-half-hour round trip five days a week. Even the club hesitated to change everything overnight and at first, while we were told to do weights in the gym during the day, the main training session was still held at six in the evening, just as it always had been.

Even the Saracens preseason tour to Scotland felt like one of the time-honoured amateur adventures, except for the fact that we were now being extremely well paid to laugh through five days of tough rugby and hard drinking. Nobody complained.

I survived my Sarries initiation, just. It started with a cocktail of Guinness, several shorts and three eggs, and continued when I was handcuffed to two senior players, Tony Copsey and John Green, and told to match them drink for drink for the rest of the night. The alcohol wasn't so bad, but the experience of having to accompany them to the toilet proved horrible. At one stage, John was having a crap in a cubicle, Tony was having a pee at the urinal and, cuffed to them both, I was stretched out between the two.

Even worse, they wouldn't let me have a pee. After two hours of holding it in, I finally persuaded to John to uncuff me from his wrist just long enough for me to unload into Tony's jacket pocket while he was ordering another round from the bar. He had no idea what was going on, but he had given me no alternative. Eventually, I had to be carried back to our hotel by the management. We didn't hold back on the field either, winning every match but, most importantly, we bonded as a squad on this paid amateur tour.

The rewards were not immediate, because we didn't settle in 1996–97 and finished fifth in the league. However, everyone stepped up a gear the following season and, inspired by Lynagh, Sella and Pienaar, we started to look and play like a formidable outfit, running neck and neck with Newcastle at the top of the table.

Our new home ground, Vicarage Road, a stadium we shared with Watford Football Club, became a fortress and, urged on by our increasingly enthusiastic and numerous fans, many of whom began turning up for games wearing the trademark red fez, we put together a powerful run in the Tetley's Bitter Cup. The club was buzzing and I was playing well, really enjoying my rugby.

Even a sore shoulder couldn't keep me out of the semifinal against Northampton and, after two painkilling injections just long enough before kick-off to keep them legal, I made two breaks that resulted in tries. We won the game and advanced to meet Wasps in the final. Our team was full of fine players but our great strength was team spirit. We backed each other unconditionally on the field, and we also had a lot of fun with each other.

I had moved to London by now and was sharing a flat with our lock forward Danny Grewcock. This worked well, even though we soon became involved in a feud with our team-mates, Paul and Richard Wallace, brothers and Irish internationals living nearby. It was me who started the problems by getting into their place and removing the labels from their tinned food, so they had no idea whether they were opening a tin of baked beans or fruit salad; then Danny stole their toothbrushes in the middle of the night.

We seemed in control, but the Wallace brothers hit back when they arranged for the guys from Sky Sports to interview them about the upcoming Tetley's final in our living room. Before the television crew arrived, they plastered the walls with every photograph of me they could lay their hands on and then, throughout the interview, the Wallies acted as though this kind of self-worship was what they had to put up with the whole time. The prank worked brilliantly, and people kept asking me if I really lived like that.

I learned soon afterwards that Danny had helped them set up the stunt, so I turned on my own flatmate and persuaded Sky to arrange a spoof trailer for the final where they would get him to dress as a Saracen warrior. I didn't believe Danny would take the bait, but he did and growled into the camera: 'Come to see the Saracens slay the Wasps.' One of the Sky TV guys then told him he had a call and handed him his mobile. Danny put the telephone to his ear, and heard me say: 'OK, mate, now we're quits.'

We prepared for the Tetley's final like true professionals. Nigel Wray paid for us to stay at a five-star hotel, and we formed a Dress Committee that arranged for the squad to be kitted out in designer suits. I also managed to get sunglasses for everyone, so we really looked like the Men in Black. All in, everything probably cost about thirty grand, but the guys felt like a million dollars when we arrived at Twickenham on an ideal sunny spring day. We sensed everything would go well when we saw the Wasps players arrive, looking a shambles in their T-shirts and tracksuits. It's sometimes said that the team that looks like professionals will play like professionals, and we were determined to prove the adage.

The players were focused as Mark Evans, our coach, ran through the tactics. I went to get another prematch injection, this time to sort out pain in my groin, and a few minutes later I had to take Aspirin as well, not for nerves but because I had a severe headache, thanks to an accidental clash with Philippe Sella.

Both the French icon and Michael Lynagh had said they would retire at the end of the season, and everyone wanted to give them a great send-off after such incredible careers. Anyway, I went up to Philippe in the changing room and just told him that I would do my very best for him. He seemed to get a bit choked up, and when the team came together in a huddle soon afterwards he said something affectionate in French – and we clashed heads.

Emotions were running high. This group might only have been together for eighteen months or so, but we were so full of the occasion, so keen to win a first trophy for the club, that in the end we all felt like Steve Ravenscroft, our centre, who was so pumped that he ran out to play with tears streaming down his face.

We wanted a fast start, and Philippe did the business, cutting through their defence to score a brilliant early try. We were up and off, and the forwards sustained the momentum with Tony Diprose, Danny and Francois Pienaar leading the way. It quickly turned into one of those dream days when every pass goes to hand, every move comes off, when you just blow your opponents right off the park. Twickenham was full and our fans were going crazy, including Nigel, who had opted to sit with his family in the stand rather than take his place with the other officials in the box.

We ran in a series of fantastic tries, and I was pleased to get over the try-line in the second half when I won a turnover ball near their 22-metre line, got round their scrum-half and swallow-dived over in the corner. There aren't many tries in my career that I can visualise as if they happened yesterday, but that's one of them. We ended up winning 48–18, collected the trophy, went ballistic and celebrated by taking three laps of honour around Twickenham.

Everyone stayed together after the game, which was great, and we drank champagne out of the cup throughout a long night that ended with more drinking and dancing at the Eros nightclub in Watford. Until today, in Sydney, which will hopefully top them all, it turned out to be the very best day of my whole career.

Michael and Philippe had gone out on a huge high and, even though Newcastle narrowly beat us to the league title, everyone felt it had been a great season. We had worked hard, together, and we had tasted the final glory, together. International rugby has a much higher profile, but there will always be something very special about winning a trophy with your mates at club level.

There was soon a double celebration in Hertfordshire

because our partners at Vicarage Road, Watford FC, won the First Division play-off final and secured promotion to the Premiership, and it was decided that both the rugby and the football team would parade through the town in open double-decker buses.

Our bus drove 100 yards behind the mighty Hornets, and we were quickly reminded how far our sport had to go before it came close to matching football's appeal. As we scanned the pavements, the loyal Sarries fans in red-and-black were massively outnumbered by the red-and-gold of the football supporters. We didn't mind and had a great time; and it was quite funny when we waved at a group of Watford fans and they just looked back at us, not quite sure what to do, clearly wondering why we were there.

The Tetley's Cup victory looked like the start of even bigger and better things for Saracens, and we were soon installed as favourites to win the league in the following season. Unfortunately, it didn't work out and, since that fantastic day at Twickenham, we have sweated through six hugely disappointing seasons. At our best, we have finished in the top five and qualified for the European Cup, and at our worst, we have flirted with relegation.

It's hard to explain this underachievement, but I believe the main factor has been the relentless turnover in players. Every new season has seemed to bring more new signings, often established internationals nearing the end of their careers, and we have battled to get any continuity or confidence within the squad. That's in contrast to a club like Leicester, who have built their team around the core of Johnson, Back, Healey and Stimpson for years.

In fact, from the Sarries squad that won the cup in 1998, Richard Hill and I are the only two still at the club; and in that period I have teamed up with no fewer than eighteen different fly-halves. With all this chopping and changing, it was always going to be difficult to fulfil the expectations of our fans, and our owner.

Nigel Wray has been extraordinarily patient over the years as he waits to see some return on his vast investment, but there have been a few occasions when he has visited the team and given us a passionate speech about how we really should be winning with all the stars we have in our team. The seasons when we have failed to qualify for Europe, and lost significant income, have been hard for him to accept, yet he still backs the club.

One time, during the depths of the dispute between the clubs and the RFU, Nigel and Francois, who was then coaching the team, called nine senior players together, outlined a dire financial situation and asked us to take a 15 per cent pay cut. Our initial response was that this was unacceptable, and we expected our binding contracts to be honoured by the club. Shocked and angry, Nigel threatened to pull his money out of the club.

In the end, we accepted a 12.5 per cent cut, on the understanding that the money saved would not be spent on new signings, so there was some surprise when Tim Horan and Thomas Castaignède arrived at the start of the next season. However, as horror stories emerged from other clubs about how guys had been picked off one-by-one to accept pay cuts, we were grateful that Nigel had been upfront with us as a group. In general, he has been an outstanding employer and the players have always appreciated his ongoing financial commitment to the club.

Off the field, at least, the club has led the way, implementing a series of creative outreach programmes in the local Hertfordshire community that have affirmed our presence and consolidated what now seems a solid fan base. I'm sure the many hundreds of school visits made by players have been worthwhile. The coaching staff and players have always worked incredibly hard to match this progress with improved results, trying every ploy and strategy, upgrading training facilities, giving us every chance to realise our potential, and we will continue to search for the formula that will bring the success the club and Nigel deserve.

In its profile, resources and outlook, Saracens should be a top-five Premiership club, challenging in the European Cup. That status has always been our ambition and I'm sure that, given the long-term commitment of everyone involved, from Nigel and the Board to the players and supporters, this will be our destiny.

Where's all the hair gone?

I'm standing in the bathroom of my hotel room, getting ready to shower and shave, looking at myself in the mirror; and, as usual, my attention is immediately drawn to the receding hairline that gets me all kind of stick from my teammates. What has happened to all that curly hair of my youth? It's just a disaster.

At least I can't blame rugby for losing my hair, not until some brilliant scientist proves beyond any doubt that relentless stress and worrying about the next big game actually does make your hair fall out. Mind you, I wouldn't be surprised if that is the case, because fourteen seasons of playing rugby has battered almost every other part of my aching body. 'Kyran Broken', mates call me. I can see why.

I stand still for a moment and assess the damage, from head to toe.

Blows to the head are commonplace in rugby, and I have had my fair share. Concussion must always be taken seriously, and only fools ignore the regulations about mandatory resting, but it can also result in funny situations because, very often, you come round and have no idea where you are or what you're doing.

In one match against Bath, Danny Grewcock caught me with a swinging arm and I was sparko for about fifteen seconds. I played on for a couple of minutes but then went up to our centre, Tim Horan, and asked him who we were playing. He said Bath but, apparently, I argued with him, insisting it was Gloucester, who we had played the previous Saturday. The physio saw I was talking gibberish and brought me off. Concussion causes short-term memory loss, but an entire week seemed to have passed me by.

Another time, I got concussed after smashing my sinus bone making a double-tackle against London Scottish. I staggered off the field and, sitting on the bench, asked our physio if he had seen my girlfriend. He laughed, and told me I had broken up with her a week before. I said that wasn't true and got quite upset with him. It was only later that night, lying in hospital, sorting out the fractures in my face, that I remembered we had indeed split up.

I have been treated on the touchline and had stitches put in a facial cut more times than I can remember, but that's normally not too bad because the adrenaline numbs the pain and, unless it's a really deep cut, you don't need an anaesthetic.

It was a bit more serious in another match between Saracens and Bath when I clashed again with Danny Grewcock, my former flatmate and good friend. Having concussed me in the same fixture the previous season, he tangled with me on the ground and one of his studs went straight through my lip. Clive Woodward was at the game and he came to see me in the changing room, thinking my jaw had been broken. Some of the guys ribbed me about that, but I was pleased to see he was so concerned.

Danny got a red card and was summoned to appear before an RFU disciplinary tribunal. He told me it had been an accident, so I attended his hearing and, even though I still didn't have any feeling in the corner of my lip, testified on his behalf. He got off and the next season I managed to complete a game against Bath without being whacked by one of my best friends in the game.

My teeth have suffered. Playing for Bristol against Bath – yes, them again – we were pressing their line when the ball popped out of a ruck. As I bent down to gather it, I collided with the head of their flanker, Andy Robinson, and my two front teeth became embedded in his scalp.

An intense, dull pain crept across my face, blood was gushing everywhere and, as I jogged across to the next ruck, I could feel air blowing into the newly mined holes in my upper gum. It was near the end, so I played on, but at the final whistle the physio took one look and said I needed a specialist. A tannoy announcement asking for a dentist to come round to the changing room brought no fewer than seven qualified dentists, all eager to help.

The consensus between them was that they should try to flip the remaining part of one tooth back into position, but they couldn't get a grip on it because I was bleeding so heavily. Somebody then produced a pair of clean garden gloves, which enabled one dentist to give it a good wrench and get it back in position. Major surgery was still required to repair my upper mouth, so I went to see my sister Jane, the dentist in Jersey. She performed miracles, and left my front teeth just about normal.

As for Andy Robinson, the Bristol team doctor stitched his wound up, but parts of my teeth were left inside his head. It all got infected, and he needed antibiotics while they slowly found their own way out of his head.

I lost my two front teeth more recently, playing for Saracens against the French side Narbonne. We were awarded a free-kick, and I wanted to take a quick tap, but one of their typically gnarled, tough, strong props walked away with the ball. *Monsieur*, I asked politely, smiling, can I have *le ballon*? He smirked back at me – and put me on the deck with a blinding head-butt.

A mass brawl followed, but the French players then insisted to the referee that I had been acting. Some act! I managed to stand up and show how my two front teeth had been dislodged from the gum and were now wedged into my gumshield. The prop was promptly sent off, and later given a sixty-day ban, which seemed just a bit longer than the time my sister Jane had to spend putting her brother's teeth back together again.

Mercifully, I haven't experienced too many problems with my neck, except for the occasional mild 'stinger'. That's the term used by rugby players to describe the feeling they get when they put in a heavy tackle and hit with part of the neck, bashing nerves that run down into your arms. Stingers make your whole arm go numb, and it sometimes takes a while for the feeling to come back, especially in your fingers. If it doesn't come back – and with me, thankfully, it always has – you need an operation to put it right.

My shoulders were absolutely fine until the day in 1997 when, having joined the Lions tour to South Africa, I was told by Keith Wood, the Irish hooker, that he could only sleep on his back because both his shoulders were too sore to take his weight. I replied by saying I had never had a problem with my shoulders. The very next day, I dislocated my right shoulder in the act of scoring a try against Northern Free State, and soon found myself back on the operating table. The doctor offered me the option of a general or a local anaesthetic. I said I wanted to stay awake, so I lay there and watched them cut me open.

They put the shoulder back in position and that was fine but, before long, I started to have trouble with my left shoulder. The AC (Acromio-Clavicular) joint kept flipping out every time I brought my hand quickly across my body, and I became quite adept at slotting it back in place. After a while, I went to see another surgeon, who was horrified by what he saw and said I needed to take a long rest.

There was no time for that, so I played on, trying to keep my shoulder safe; and I managed to do that until the last match of the 1997–98 season when, playing for Saracens against Northampton, I put in a tackle and felt the whole shoulder rupture. It was absolute agony, but the pain subsided in the changing room and that night I was feeling fine. In fact, I seemed to have more movement in the joint and I could stretch my arm right across my body. X-rays later showed the ligament attaching the AC joint to the collarbone had snapped and there was now no need for an operation.

'Popped ribs' is a condition that occurs when some form of impact literally 'pops' one rib out of line with the others. The result is exceptional pain, something like the worst imaginable heartburn, particularly when you breathe in. Forwards tend to suffer this injury more than backs, but I have often popped my ribs, most painfully in a match against Ireland in 2001. It happened soon after I came on as a substitute for Matt Dawson, so there was nobody left on the bench who could come on for me. I was crunching in agony every time I passed, but there was no option but to play on and somehow get through to the end of the match.

At one stage of my career, a recurring groin injury threatened to become as much of a nightmare as my back problems, but Dan Luger, my England team-mate, introduced me to something called 'Skinnar', an electromagnetic treatment specially developed for Russian astronauts, and the problem was solved.

It started when, waking up one morning, I suddenly found it hard to walk and almost impossible to change direction at speed. A specialist took a look at me, sticking his finger right up into my scrotum to feel if there were any holes between the pelvis and the muscle belly. He reckoned I had a hernia and needed an operation. So I had that done and, although I couldn't stand up straight for a month, I was back playing rugby within six weeks.

The groin still wasn't right, though. I played on, as most players do when they have an injury that is just annoying and sore rather than debilitating and downright agony, but the condition was affecting my performance. A year later I saw a second specialist and another highly trained finger plunged deep into my scrotum. This time it returned with the disconcerting verdict that I required the insertion of a wire mesh, which would get knitted into the tissue in my groin and hopefully strengthen the whole area. It sounded like a great idea, so I had that done, but, again, the effects were negligible and I played with a painful groin for two more years.

Sometimes it was fine, other times it was sore, but it was always there, always holding me back, always denying me the kind of free, easy movement every player craves. Just as the situation was getting me down, to a point where it was threatening to finish my career, Dan told me how Skinnar had helped him overcome a similar problem. The Russians had apparently wanted to develop a system that would help their astronauts recover from ailments in space without needing to take tablets, and their solution was this machine that sent electric pulses to stimulate and regenerate the nervous system in the affected part of the body.

I was willing to give it a try, especially when Dan added that the doctor running the Skinnar treatment sessions in London was a particularly attractive Russian lady, who didn't appear to have any qualms about telling him to strip off so she could start treating the most personal areas of his body. So I went along and, after a while, it seemed that rubbing the instrument over one particular area of my groin, sending electric shocks into the nerves, certainly eased the pain. I should point out this treatment was not quite as much fun as it sounds, but the plain medical fact is that, after three or four visits, my groin felt better than it had in years. 'I don't think you'll need any more treatment down there,' said the doctor, and she was right.

Touch wood, my knees haven't given me too many problems though the years, although I did have one operation on my right knee when acute pain in one area was eased by the removal of what the surgeon described as the biggest cyst he had ever seen. I also tore my medial ligaments once, when one Frenchman tackled me from the left at the same moment as another tackled me from the right. There was a snapping sound at impact and, when I tried to carry on, it felt as though I was running on stilts.

Six weeks in a full leg brace put me right, but my period

Top Jamie Joseph, whose boot left me hobbling throughout my debut, looms large as I try to get the ball away. (*Colorsport*)

Above The England team celebrates after beating New Zealand 15–9 in November 1993. (*Colorsport*)

Right After the game, and celebrating my first cap in style with a can of Foster's Export.

With Dewi Morris, my first main rival for the England scrum-half role, in March 1994. It was that month I got my first, but not last, experience of being dropped. (*Colorsport*)

Mike Catt, Neil Back, Richard West and I practise our surfing on the beach in Durban ahead of our first game in the World Cup in May 1995. There was more time for such things in those amateur days. (*Empics*)

Danny Grewcock, Mike Catt and I lead the way into training at Sandhurst on 22 November 2000 as we try to get things back to normal after the threatened players' strike that week. (*David Rogers/Getty Images*)

Discussing tactics with Clive Woodward during our North American tour of 2001. Wherever possible, Woodward left nothing to chance. (*Colorsport*)

Opposite February 1998 and I score a try in our record 60–26 victory over Wales. Jeremy Guscott looks on with a smile, knowing just how unusual this was for me in an England shirt. (*Empics*)

The England team 'celebrate' winning the Six Nations in October 2001, after Ireland prevented us from gaining a Grand Slam. (*Colorsport*)

Martin Johnson survives a training ground encounter with me. Towards the end of my career, I began to develop a reputation for leaving players injured after bizarre accidents. (*Colorsport*)

Gareth Thomas forces a knock-on when he came up from an offside position to tackle me in our match in February 2003. On such small decisions are places in a side won and lost. (*Empics*)

Another year, another Grand Slam decider in Dublin. The result in 2003 was much better and our 42–6 victory meant that Clive Woodward was already setting the next target: winning the World Cup. (*Colorsport*)

Summer 2003, and Jonny Wilkinson and I combine to tackle Richard McCaw in our 15–13 victory. (*Empics*)

'I'm fine, honest.' My team-mates look on during the World Cup warm-up game against France in September 2003. There was no way I wasn't getting on that plane to Australia. (*Empics*)

Matt Dawson and I prepare to battle it out for the No. 9 shirt in the World Cup. (*Colorsport*)

Training with Jonny Wilkinson ahead of the game against Uruguay. If ever a player proved that you take out of the game what you put in, it is Jonny, whose professionalism is quite remarkable. (*Empics*)

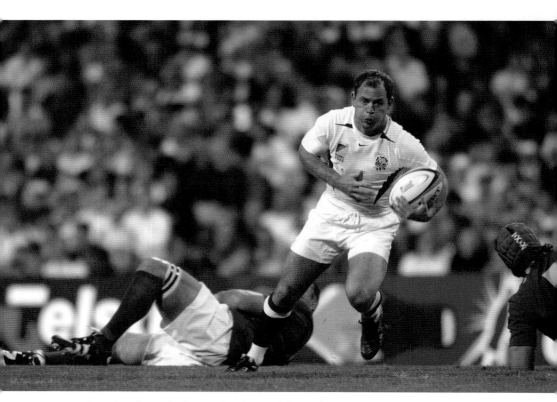

Bursting through the South African defence during our crucial Group decider. I was pleased with my form, but was rested for the next game and lost my position in the starting line-up for good. (*Colorsport*)

Martin Johnson was too exhausted even to raise a smile after playing in the World Cup, but his inspirational leadership was immense.

Richard Hill lets it all sink in after England are crowned world champions.

Friends Paul and Pam Bell, brother-in-law David Jenkins, Dad, sister Jane, Mum and brother John. Jane and David made a round-trip of fifty-six hours to be there. That's commitment!

Victoria couldn't travel to Australia for the World Cup, because she was so heavily pregnant at the time, but she did manage to get her hands on the trophy when we returned with it.

Little sister Louise, who has supported me through thick and thin over the years.

Richard Hill is the man left holding the Cup during our parade through London. Jonny Wilkinson, Mark Regan and I look on. (*Empics*)

Receiving a silver cap to mark fifty caps for England before the Barbarians game against England in December 2003. Jonny Wilkinson, who had also reached the same landmark looks on. It was my last appearance in an England shirt at Twickenham.

of convalescence was not helped when my flatmate at the time, Danny Grewcock, suffered the same injury a week later. People laughed out loud when they saw us shopping in the supermarket, both in leg braces, limping in tandem, squeaking in chorus.

Running on hard ground is generally the cause of shin splints, extremely painful tiny fractures all along the shin. Normal treatment is a course of anti-inflammatories and an ice bath, where you have to sit with your feet and shins in a bucket of ice and water. If this was not a form of ancient torture, it should have been, but, during one quiet afternoon with the England squad, we organised a contest to see who could stay in an ice bath for the longest time. I emerged as the winner, shivering, with a time of fourteen minutes.

The big toe may not seem a particularly vulnerable part of the anatomy, although footballer Gary Lineker would probably have a different opinion because his career was ended by a big toe injury. I suffered from something called 'turf toe', which happens when you stub the toe while it is in flexion. It is unbelievably painful and, for four or five weeks afterwards, I could hardly run without getting the doctor to give me a painkilling injection.

That's where the real agony starts, because there is no more awkward place to have an injection than the big toe. The doctor has to pull the central joint apart and then insert the needle at a certain angle. On several occasions, it took three or four attempts to get it right, by which time I was rolling around in pain.

Turf toe was not much fun, but it was nothing compared to the recurring injury that has most affected my career. My notorious glass back has almost always been a problem, forcing me to miss matches, giving me sleepless nights. How many long hours have I spent lying in pain, cursing my back? I lost count long ago. Looking back, I can't recall the drawn-out saga of many different diagnoses and treatments, but certain images endure . . .

In 1988, aged eighteen, starting at Bristol University, eager to play and show I'm worthy of the bursary, I get a sharp pain in my lower back and think it's nothing. It isn't nothing. In fact, I've torn a disc, which means scar tissue starts to form around the lower lumbar discs at level four and five of my spine. Every knock will produce more scar tissue, until I get what they call a bulging disc, and that could be a problem, but I feel OK and play on . . .

In 1997, after eight years of intermittent pain, I am working through fitness testing with the England squad and a fitness adviser wants me to do squats with a 125kg bar. I tell him it's too much for my back. He reckons I'm messing around. I say I'm not and offer to do more repetitions with a lighter weight. He's not listening, and repeats the instruction. I'm upset. I hate this.

I manage five reps, and then feel a shooting pain in my back, drop the weight and scream out loud. The fitness adviser is telling me he's sorry, but it's a bit late for that, mate. The doctor's verdict is a torn disc that rules me out of Saturday's international against South Africa and another six weeks after that. I can't move without pain, and I can hardly stand up straight. When I ought to be in my prime, this back makes me look and feel like an old man . . .

In 1999, touring Australia as preparation for the World Cup, my back starts to feel sore while I am training, doing some sprints on a rubber track. I stop for a moment, decide it's not too bad and play in the Test against Australia at the Olympic Stadium. The pain gets worse during the match, and I have to leave the field during the second half. We lose the game and I am in agony. It becomes so bad at the post-match reception that the only way I can get any relief is to lie down on the hard floor. People are watching me. What are they thinking? I'm in too much pain to care.

Back in England, racing to get fit in time for the World Cup, I see an orthopaedic surgeon who suggests using an epidural needle to shoot anti-inflammatory chemicals up my spinal cord. He thinks this could reduce the swelling around the discs. The needle is a foot long, and I have to look away when it goes in. It doesn't really help, so they try the same procedure a week later. The improvement is minimal, but he says we should do it a third time.

'If this doesn't work,' the specialist says, 'we'll have to fortify your lower back with bone from your hip. It's called a fusion, and it could make it difficult for you to bend. I have to say your chances of playing top-class rugby again are very slim.'

I am devastated, disbelieving. In tears, I phone Victoria – then my girlfriend, now my wife – and tell her what the doctor says. She is strong and urges me to stay calm. It's not easy.

Saracens send me to see an insurance assessor, who agrees with the first diagnosis and says he doesn't think I will ever be able to play rugby again. Don't give up the day job, he jokes as I leave his room. Does he know what he's saying? This is my life. I'm only twenty-eight years old. Why is this happening? I travel home on the London Underground, but am so dazed and dumbfounded that I stay on the train three stops too far. What do I look like? Everything seems to be falling apart. My whole world is crumbling.

Victoria is fantastic. She keeps me going, keeps me hoping. We decide to rule out a fusion and start looking for alternative forms of treatment. There must be a solution. I'm not giving up. I want to keep playing rugby. I want to take part in the World Cup. I ignore the medical advice. I refuse to give up.

First, I go to see Ron Holder, a London-based South African kinesiologist who has helped many top athletes recover from injury by using an unusual combination of deep massage and correcting the balance of your body by putting appropriately sized bits of telephone directory in your left and right shoe. Many rugby players swear by him, but I have only limited success.

Next, I am standing in front of Mark Zambarda, an athletics coach with a reputation for helping people like me who have come to a dead end with conventional medicine. He uses his entire body weight to get into the deep muscle fibres, and he works on my mind by asking me to visualise running without pain, and he even gets me to do some back squats with severe pain, but nothing is getting better and the World Cup is getting closer.

Third, I go to see Eileen Drewery, the faith healer who has become famous for her work with Glenn Hoddle, the former England football manager. She puts her hands on my back and keeps them there for half an hour, looking as though she is praying, silently. Then she gives me a cup of tea, and that's it. I'm not a massive believer in this kind of thing, but my back does seem to improve, so I decide to meet with Eileen a few more times.

One day I turn up and find a whole crowd of journalists and photographers gathered outside her house. Glenn

Hoddle is there, seeking help through some problems in his marriage, and I spend some time talking to him and Eileen. I don't necessarily agree with all their views, but they are two of the most decent people you could ever wish to meet. After a while, Glenn offers to give me a lift to the station, and I find him really sympathetic.

I'm still not right, but there is one more chance. One of the leading microsurgeons in Britain, John Webb, of Nottingham, injects chymopapain into the bulging disc and tries to dissolve it from the inside out. I start feeling really sore on the train back to London and, arriving at Paddington station, I am in such a bad way that I have to be met on the platform, lifted onto the back of a cart and driven at three miles per hour to the taxi rank. This soon becomes embarrassing because, as the driver shouts to clear the way, people recognise me and start to chuckle at the sight of an England rugby player needing to be treated in this way. It doesn't take long for me to realise this latest injection has not really worked. Everything has been in vain, and I am forced to accept my back will keep me out of the 1999 World Cup.

An operation now seems unavoidable, but on inspecting my back for a second time, John Webb reckons he could shave the disc rather than fuse it. This less intrusive surgery is better than a fusion because it will give me the opportunity to make a complete recovery and play rugby again. Shall we try? he asks. Of course, I reply. On 12 September 1999, I go under his knife.

Everything goes well on the day, but that's the easy part. The real challenge lies in staying disciplined through nearly five months of rehabilitation, driving myself through mind-numbing exercises for up to six hours every day. If I do them, I'll make a complete recovery and play rugby again. If I don't, I'll struggle. It's hard, it's indescribably boring, and it just has to be done . . .

I am fit. After being told, twice, that I might never play rugby again, after ten and a half months out of the game, I am ready to play for Saracens against Newcastle. My back feels good. Barely two minutes into the match, I look up and see the powerful figure of Va'aiga Tuigamala bearing down on me. There's no escape. I don't need an escape. I tackle him, no bother. I'm OK.

The memories of this long-running saga make me shudder, even though I have gradually learned to live with the awareness that my back could go at any time, just as it went before our opening game of this World Cup, against Georgia. How close do I come to disaster every time I bend down? I really don't know.

Sometimes, just playing with my back in this fragile condition feels like walking on eggshells. Well, if that's true, after all these years, after all the pain and desperate days, I reckon I've got pretty good at walking on eggshells. My back feels 100 per cent this morning, no problem at all. How will it feel when I am fifty years old? I don't care. Right now, it only has to be fine for the match tonight.

So, still standing here in the bathroom of my hotel room, still staring at myself in the mirror, it's not difficult to understand why I seem to have earned a reputation for being injury-prone, but I don't accept it as true. Reputations are hard to shake off in professional sport – you get a label, you live with it – but the fact is that in eleven years of senior rugby I have played 220 league matches, at least another sixty friendlies and fifty-one internationals. That's an average of over thirty games per year, which is pretty respectable, especially when you think my back injury kept me out for a year.

One more game: that's all this body needs to get me through. Some days, I feel as if I have had enough . . . enough of the aches and the physical battering, enough of the pressure, enough of being away from home and missing my wife, enough of being told what to do. I haven't said anything to anyone, not to Clive or any member of the management but, somewhere at the back of my mind, I think this will be it.

On the other hand, as the old cliché goes, you're a long time retired, and I make a decent living from this game. It may be stupid to stop the car when I've still got petrol in the tank. That decision will wait for another day. Right now, I feel fine.

There's no point hanging around in my hotel room when I'm up and about, so I decide to head down to breakfast, even if that means I might be the first one there. It's now just after eight o'clock in the morning. Some of the guys, those able to sleep late even on this most nerve-racking day, won't appear until ten.

I'm not the first. Clive is there. As I walk into the dining room, I notice the coach holding forth, sitting with members of his carefully selected management team. He looks excited, full of ideas, bursting with enthusiasm, full of chat, just as he has looked almost every day since he accepted the England job in 1997.

'Good morning, KB,' he says, cheerily.

'Morning, Clive,' I say, moving along to find another empty table on the opposite side of the room. The management are the management; players are players. We get along just fine but we do tend to eat with our own kind. I get my usual fruit and yoghurt from the self-service counter and settle down, eating quietly, every now and then stealing a glance across at the coach.

I remember how, not long after his appointment, he called the top sixty players in the country to a meeting at Bisham Abbey. There had been some grumbling that he had only coached at London Irish and Bath, and that he might not have sufficient experience to succeed at international level, but most of us were prepared to give him the benefit of the doubt because he had a strong playing background, which was an advantage over Jack Rowell. Rugby players can be a highly demanding and critical audience, but we were at least going to listen to a former international who had won twenty-one caps for England in the 1980s, including the Grand Slam in 1980, and played for the Lions in 1980, as well as touring with them in 1983.

'My main aim is to win the 1999 World Cup,' he said, with a bluntness that we would grow to adore, 'and, to do that, we'll need the strongest, fastest and fittest team in the world.'

That was fine, but Clive then launched into a demonstration of a particular weight-training programme, using players to show the various techniques. This went on and on. People were beginning to get restless and, after more than an hour, there was a rush for the door when we were finally allowed to leave.

The verdict on the coach was mixed. Some guys reckoned the weights thing was strange, but others liked him. I said I thought his straight-speaking, businesslike manner was exactly what the England team needed. That's what I told anyone who asked, but the real reason I liked Clive from the start was that I had been led to believe that he rated me as a scrum-half. That is all any player ever wants from his coach, to feel supported.

In fact, it was a shame Clive hadn't been appointed to coach the Lions to South Africa in 1997, because he might have selected me in the original squad. Missing out on that tour had been one of the biggest disappointments of my career. The Lions are special and, even though I did later get called out as a replacement when Rob Howley dislocated his shoulder, and I scored a try in my solitary appearance in the red jersey, against Northern Free State, I was still upset not to have been involved from the start. Martin Johnson had been a great captain, uniting the Irish, Scots, English and Welsh, and forging a great spirit in the squad.

That was all in the past but the future looked bright if the new coach thought I was a decent player. Looking back over the past six years, I can reflect that this early optimism has been justified. Clive has supported me, not to the exclusion of other scrum-halves, but I have almost always been in or around his England squad.

I glance across the dining room once again, and the coach is laughing at something, looking confident and assured. He has come such a long way and now, this morning, he stands on the brink of a massive achievement, of being placed on the same pedestal as Sir Alf Ramsey, as coach of a World Cup-winning England team. If we do beat the Australians tonight, they'll probably knight him as well. Will we call him Sir Clive? I chuckle at the thought.

As I sit there eating breakfast on my own, I decide there are probably three main reasons for his success.

The first sounds dull and predictable, but he has an incredible work ethic. It is true that as the first full-time, professional England coach he is the first to have had the opportunity to commit himself in mind and body to the job, but it is the heart and soul he puts into his work that his successors will struggle to match. It is not unusual to find Clive and his assistants up at five in morning, talking about players' strengths and weaknesses, watching videos to see what works and what doesn't, planning training sessions.

As he puts in the hours, so his attention to detail is amazing. Every single aspect of every match we play is analysed, discussed and either confirmed or amended. Nothing is ever left to chance, left unsaid or left undone. Everyone talks about getting that extra 1 per cent of performance, but Clive wants it first.

There are literally hundreds of examples, but one is his decision to include a full-time referee as a member of our squad during the week before an international. This man's job is solely to study the referee who has been appointed to handle the match and brief us on his habits and preferences. Coaches typically shrug their shoulders and say they can't do much about the officials, but Clive is not typical. He sets to work and devises a system that empowers his team to run onto the field aware of what they can do, what they must not do and what they may get away with.

Secondly, he has an ability to look at the game in a different way from everyone else and, of equal importance, he has the talent to communicate his thoughts to his players.

His vision is total rugby, a game where front-row forwards can sidestep like Jason Robinson, where second-row forwards can pass accurately from the base of a ruck and where the back row are able to fill in at centre. Critics have suggested he is attempting to turn the union game into a hybrid of rugby league, but that is nonsense. Aside from the fact that no sport with such diverse features as the contested scrum and the line-out will ever be one-dimensional, Clive wants to take the game to a different level.

To do that, as he said at that first meeting at Bisham Abbey, he needs players who are strong, fast and skilful. All our training is dedicated to achieving that goal and, while we are certainly not the perfect team – short of cloning fifteen Richard Hills, that is probably unattainable, even for Clive – I think the current England side is as close to his concept as any in the world today.

He doesn't coach from any dog-eared manual or from what he picks up on the Internet ... he talks about things like 'T-Cup', which is Thinking Correctly Under Pressure, a mental exercise designed to help us make the right decisions at the most important moments of the most important matches. There have been times when he would sit us all down in front of a video of some game, and pause the tape at a pivotal moment, for example when we have a scrum on their line.

'Right,' he would say, 'this is the situation. There's no time left. We have to score. What call do you make?'

'Jack Knife,' someone might suggest.

He would counter: 'Jack Knife? Why would you do that? Why on earth do you think that would work?'

We would explain our logic, and he would challenge it, and put us under pressure, and make us think.

'Would you bet your life on that call?' he would say.

Session by session, we have become familiar with these types of high-pressure situations, so when we face them in a match, we'll be equipped to cope, and make the right decision.

Once, he talked about the six 'f's, where we were told to

read a piece of text and count the number of 'f's that we saw. Most of the players quickly came up with three as the answer but, told to look again, we noticed that in fact there were six 'f's. 'You see,' Clive said with a grin, 'anyone can see the obvious. The difference between winning and losing is the ability to see what is not obvious.'

Not everyone understood what he was saying, and through all his ideas and exercises there have been times when the consensus within the squad was that Clive was stark raving bonkers but, more often than not, the penny eventually dropped.

At one point in our preparations for the 1999 World Cup, the coach organised a kind of treasure trail where we were all given a series of clues to decipher. He said the forwards would compete as one team against the backs. It was raining on this afternoon but the forwards charged off with their sheet of clues, running all over the estate to find the treasure. Meanwhile, the backs sat down under cover and quietly studied the clues. After a while, one of the guys realised the last letter of each clue combined to make an anagram of the word 'boathouse'. We had discovered the answer and won the contest without getting wet.

The forwards eventually returned, drenched and exhausted, and they did look as though they wanted to eat our heads off when they were told what had happened. It's the six 'f's, we teased them, and Clive laughed as well. Day by day, we were starting to think in the way he wanted us to think.

Another occasion, during England's summer tour to Australia in 1999, the coach called the team's decision-makers to a meeting and, as soon as we had sat down, he asked how many drop goals we thought we could get in a single match.

'Bothered?' replied Mike Catt, thinking the coach was making some kind of joke. He wasn't. Straight-faced, Clive asked what he meant by that, and Catty just about crawled out of the situation by saying it was like asking how long is a piece of string.

'Seriously,' the coach insisted, 'if we went into an important match against top-class opposition with the sole aim of getting into their half and kicking drop goals, without even attempting to score a try, how many do you think we would get?'

We were starting to look at each other blankly, reckoning this was another moment when Clive's blue-sky thinking had gone into another galaxy, and eventually answered four or five.

'No,' he snapped. 'We would get eleven or twelve. That would give us thirty-six points, enough to win most big matches.'

Our meeting ended soon afterwards. Barely four months later, we were knocked out of the 1999 Rugby World Cup when we lost a massively disappointing quarter-final in Paris to South Africa, whose fly-half, Jannie de Beer, kicked a record five drop goals. Back then, we weren't completely in tune with Clive's thinking. I think we have improved now and tonight, here in Sydney, will be the proof.

The third reason for the coach's success has been his absolute commitment to treating the players well. Often repeating his belief that superstar treatment would produce superstar performances, he has regularly squeezed the last drop of funding from the RFU to provide us with the perfect environment to realise our potential. Just before his appointment in 1997, the England squad flew to Argentina in Economy Class, with 6' 5" second-row forwards being asked to sit doubled up for a twenty-hour flight. Under Clive, there is no debate: wherever we go, we travel Business Class.

In the past, the players' wives or girlfriends were expected to make their own arrangements on match days, often causing hassle for players, who had to spend time and energy making sure things were organised. Was the ticket fixed? Could she collect the parking pass? It frequently became a nightmare. Clive changed everything. He realised our partners endure many of the same pressures as us, and brought them under the same England tent.

All of a sudden, they were being recognised, receiving gifts of perfume, scarves and clothing, and being invited to private drinks parties on the days before international matches. Jane Woodward, Clive's wife, took care to make everyone feel welcome and involved, and the RFU was even persuaded to provide special supervised play facilities where players could take their children. It was simple stuff: happy, involved partner generally equals happy, relaxed player equals optimum performance. Clive worked it out, devised the systems and made sure they worked.

He also looked after us. In the past, successive generations of England players had sensed every item of kit or equipment, every match ticket and privilege was grudgingly offered by a Union whose top officials seemed to subscribe to the old adage that rugby would be a great game if it wasn't for the players. Under Clive, the players were unquestionably the No. 1 priority and we didn't have to ask for anything: each member of the squad was given a mobile phone, a designer suit, a personal computer and much more.

Certain administrators clearly believed Clive went too far and, at one point, they seized upon our use of personal computers as an innovation that wasn't working. The coach's idea had been to create an online forum, restricted to management and players, where we would be able to communicate with each other, posting schedules, discussing tactics and even announcing teams.

Problems arose on days when everyone knew the team was going to be announced. Some players wouldn't be able to get online to check their e-mail, so they started to phone their team-mates to see if they had received news of the team, and the entire process quickly became chaotic and uncomfortable.

The electronic system also seemed impersonal. Some players said that if they had been dropped, they would prefer to be told in person, and it did sometimes feel strange to be clicking post-match comments into the ether rather than speaking in a meeting where you could judge the general mood of the squad. It was easy to be too honest, say the wrong thing and cause trouble.

After losing to Australia in 1999, all of the players were told to e-mail their personal thoughts on our performance to Clive within twenty-four hours. I sent him a message in which I said I thought we had lost because we went into the match without really believing we could win. It was only when I got a quick reply from Clive asking me to explain what I meant that I realised I had been referring to events in a meeting he didn't know about.

What had happened was that, before the game, Johnno had called a private meeting for the players alone, and that was where various speakers had left me with the impression that we generally lacked self-belief. Now I had no option but to tell Clive what had taken place. He was furious, not just because he had been excluded but also because of what had been said. The coach promptly forwarded my e-mail to the rest of the squad, leaving me feeling like an idiot and looking like the school snitch. This triggered a torrent of abuse from my team-mates, and it took me some months to live that one down.

Clive eventually stopped using the computers for this purpose, but I think his idea will prove to have been ahead of its time. With a few refinements, a restricted electronic network will surely become the most effective method of team communications.

A work ethic, a clear vision and a commitment to put players first: this is what Clive brought to his job and, under this calibre of leadership, it is no surprise that the England team have been so successful during the past six years. Perhaps the most worthwhile measure of our progress is the recent improvement in our results against the three southern-hemisphere powers.

As I've mentioned before, for most of the 1990s, we were simply overwhelmed by New Zealand, Australia and South Africa. Aside from a few triumphant afternoons at Twickenham, one great win in Pretoria in 1994 and the 1995 World Cup quarter-final victory over Australia, these giants of the game ran all over us. I have sat in my fair share of battered England changing rooms, feeling as though we had been flattened by a train, wondering what happened.

Their superiority was partly physical. Whether or not it was the sunshine or their outdoor culture, something made the southern-hemisphere players bigger, stronger and faster. Some of the South African forwards were so enormous they seemed to be a different species altogether and, whether they had adopted the colours of the All Blacks or the Wallabies, a succession of South Sea Islanders proved almost impossible to contain and stop.

There was also a gulf in basic skills. One glance at action from the regional Super 12 or the Tri-Nations, the main annual southern-hemisphere competitions launched at the start of professional rugby in 1996, revealed a pace and quality in all positions that simply did not exist in the northern hemisphere.

Third, we were essentially playing a different game. Whereas southern-hemisphere referees regularly played the advantage law and kept the game moving, our rugby tended to plod from set piece to set piece. While they were spinning the ball around the field, we were contesting leaden wars of attrition in the scrums, the rucks and the mauls. It was predictable that when the two systems clashed we would be made to look like carthorses chasing thoroughbreds. In our tactics, in physical fitness, in mental preparation, we really were a breed apart.

Clive recognised the nature of the challenge and resolutely set out to close the gap by (1) putting his players into a fitness regime that would make them equally big, strong and fast, (2) relentlessly improving the skills levels of his team to a point where the forwards could operate as backs, and vice versa, and (3) coaching England to play a high-tempo, fast and fluent brand of rugby, and yet retain their ability to keep things tight when required.

His strategy has worked. Since the 1999 World Cup, we have turned Twickenham into a fortress, defeating South Africa on their last four visits and the Wallabies on their last three. In addition, victories in Bloemfontein, Wellington and Melbourne have put an end to any fears that we cannot win away from home. In fact, as we stand today, the general consensus around the world is that Woodward's England side has not just caught up with the southern-hemisphere giants, but may even have edged ahead.

I'm not so sure. Perhaps we can reasonably be ranked on the same level as the big three. On our day, we'll beat them. On their day, they'll beat us. Either way, we still have huge respect for three great teams, each with their own unique appeal.

The Springboks are always physical, always committed and probably the biggest hitters. Every time I've played against them, I have been black and blue the next morning, covered in bruises and aching all over. When you get tackled by a South African, you tend to stay tackled for the next week or so.

Nobody knew much about the Springboks when they emerged from isolation in 1992, but they had settled within three years and their 1995 team were worthy world champions. They came to play at Twickenham five months after winning the World Cup, and beat us quite convincingly. I had been warned to watch their scrum-half, Joost van der Westhuizen, and was told that he only ever breaks on the left. Well, he was big and strong, and he scored a fantastic try sprinting clear down the right touchline.

We continued to struggle against the Springboks for the next few years, at home and away, but the balance of power in our ongoing rivalry seemed to change when we played in Bloemfontein in 2000. The England team going into this particular Test match was as pumped up and motivated as any I have known. We felt robbed and annoyed, and downright bloody-minded.

The robbery had taken place in the first Test in Pretoria when Tim Stimpson appeared to be blocked when he followed up a kick to score what would have been a match-winning try. Some of the guys reckoned he had still managed to get the touchdown, but at least we should have had a penalty or a penalty try. The referee gave us nothing, disgracefully, and we were beaten 18–13.

We were also annoyed because the Springboks were allowed to abuse the blood-replacement rule. One of their players had come off the field during the second half, supposedly because he was bleeding, but we couldn't see any blood. Ten minutes later, after a nice rest to recharge his batteries, he came back and rampaged around for the last twenty minutes. While we were being the jolly good English, respecting the letter of the laws, our opponents were doing pretty much what they liked. If we were to be competitive against these teams, Clive and the senior players quickly realised we would have to become equally adept at bending the laws.

So we trained for the second Test with that air of desperation that is so valuable in a sporting team. You can't manufacture it, and you can't coach it. It's usually triggered by something an opponent has said or done, or a bad refereeing decision, or a combination of circumstances. It just materialises now and then, and it happened in Bloemfontein. Nothing was going to stop us.

Nothing did stop us. We played with a perfect blend of passion and control, which was neatly captured in one moment when Austin Healey bravely scampered back to retrieve the ball behind our own line, sidestepped two charging Springboks and calmly kicked the ball into touch. I played my part when I held Corne Krige up as he stormed over our try-line, and Jonny, recovered from the illness that had kept him out of the first Test, was outstanding.

Our 27–22 victory was a crucial moment in the development of this England side. We had proved to ourselves we could beat one of the great southern-hemisphere teams on their own turf. We had proved the years of regular hammerings were over. That evening in Bloemfontein, as the celebratory beer flooded our senses, self-belief flooded through the squad. We could compete with the best teams in the world. We could beat anybody. We knew it.

New Zealand are unique opponents because whenever you line up against the All Blacks you have a very keen sense of playing against the entire country. Whether you're in Auckland, Wellington, Christchurch or anywhere, everyone seems to know who you are, what you are doing and by how many points you're going to get beaten by their unrivalled national heroes.

This kind of fanatical support can be counterproductive when it piles pressure on the players but, at its best, it underpins the aura that surrounds this team. The black kit, the haka, the pride in the silver fern on the jersey: it looks impressive from the stands, and it looks awesome from the other side of halfway.

I was fortunate to be part of the England team that beat the All Blacks in 1993 – international debuts don't come any better than that – but we struggled to get a result against them through the rest of the decade. Their superiority was most vividly confirmed at Old Trafford in 1997. They won the game 25–8, but we had been so impressed by the fantastic support from the Manchester crowd that we decided to do a lap of honour after the game. With hindsight, it probably wasn't a clever thing to do, and it felt quite embarrassing when the New Zealanders were quoted in the Sunday newspapers, saying we had looked pathetic celebrating a defeat.

Just two weeks later, playing them again at Twickenham, we thought we had turned everything around when we stormed into a big lead, but they irrepressibly ground their way back and a great match finished as a 26–26 draw.

So we generally continued to suffer until we travelled to play the All Blacks in Wellington earlier this year. The memory of that 15–13 victory is fresh in our minds, and it is the vivid images of our pack of forwards standing up to theirs, and our defensive system keeping their back line in check.

The Australians are special opponents because, over the past twenty years or so, they have developed a knack of winning tight games in the dying minutes. Some people have said they're lucky, but their last-gasp heroics are too frequent for fortune to be a factor. In my opinion, it is an unshakable self-belief, an iron mental strength that drives them through the white-knuckle moments.

The Aussies have obviously produced some special talents as well, such as David Campese, but it is their strutting self-confidence that we must match. That will be the key tonight. They will run out to play absolutely believing they are going to win. Will we? I think we will. That's how far we have come.

Improving results against the big three gradually raised public expectations ahead of our Six Nations campaigns. If we beat all, or even two, of the All Blacks, Wallabies and Springboks in the autumn internationals at Twicken-ham, it was automatically assumed that we would go on and ease to another Grand Slam. In practice, over the past few years, life hasn't been so straightforward.

Glancing across the dining room at Clive, I see he is still at breakfast, still chatting to his assistants, still smiling. He looks happy now, but he didn't look so pleased at Wembley in 1999 when we needed only to beat Wales to win the

Grand Slam, and lost; nor at Murrayfield in 2000, when we had to beat Scotland to take the Grand Slam, and lost; nor at Lansdowne Road in 2001, when we needed to beat Ireland to claim the Grand Slam, and lost.

Three years in succession, we were able to taste the big prize in northern-hemisphere rugby. Three times, we choked. While we were so impressively making up ground on our modern rivals in the southern hemisphere, it's strange that we were so regularly pegged back by traditional adversaries closer to home.

Injury kept me out of the 1999 match against Wales – I had torn a knee ligament in our victory over France – and I was gutted, but an invitation to be a panel guest for the BBC TV coverage of the match seemed like some kind of consolation. However, as the day unfolded, I suffered as much of a nightmare up in the studio as my team-mates were enduring down on the field.

Everyone connected with the England squad was feeling quite confident as we arrived at Wembley, which the Welsh were using as a temporary home while the Millennium Stadium was being built in Cardiff, and I felt bold enough to tease my fellow panellist, Jonathan Davies, the former Wales fly-half, that I stood to make £10,000 as an England player's bonus for winning the Grand Slam while he was getting only £500 for a day's work with the BBC.

The first half proved tighter than anyone expected, but during the half-time break I confidently assured the television audience of millions that Wales would tire as the game wore on and England would win by twenty points. Jonathan didn't say much until, with about ten minutes remaining, and the match still too tight for comfort, he turned to me with a grin and said: 'Listen, Kyran, I'll bet you my BBC fee that Wales score in the last few minutes, and then you'll be able to stick your team bonus right up your arse.'

I agreed, and then watched in horror as Wales won a penalty, kicked to the corner, went off the top and whipped the ball to Scott Gibbs, who cut us to pieces, sidestepping his way through to score. Neil Jenkins kicked the conversion and Wales had won. As Wembley erupted in red joy, Jonathan went berserk, cheering, jumping all over me and burying my head in his arms.

A few moments later, the red light on the camera switched on and Steve Rider started the panel discussion. I was trying to be as magnanimous as possible in defeat but as I spoke I noticed on the studio monitor that, following the scuffle with Jonathan, the collar of my shirt was overlapping my jacket. I looked a right idiot, and tried to put it right without anyone noticing. However, the monitor shows a reflected image, so I reached for the collar on my left when it was the right side that needed fixing. Jonathan looked ready to burst out laughing, and I felt like even more of a fool.

Switching on my mobile after the broadcast finished, I found at least fifteen messages asking me why I had looked so scruffy on national television. It hadn't been a great day.

Twelve months later, we approached the Grand Slam decider in Edinburgh with caution. I was injured again, in the midst of my long lay-off with a back injury, and Johnno was also out, so Matt Dawson captained the side. Daws is a friend of mine, and we have always got along, but he has also been my rival for the England No. 9 jersey, and the reality of professional sport is that you never want your rival to play well. Not many people are willing to admit that, but everyone knows it's true. You desperately want the team to win, but you want the guy in your position to have a shocker. I'm sure Daws feels the same when I play.

So, sitting at home, with my back aching, watching the match against Scotland on television, I wasn't too excited by the prospect of seeing my rival stepping forward to collect the Six Nations trophy as England captain, bathed in glory and, in the process, sending me even further into the wilderness. That said, I desperately wanted the guys to triumph, not least because I believed Clive deserved the reward of a major trophy for all his hard work.

Unfortunately, the Scots hassled and harassed as if their lives depended on the match. The game became a dogfight, we lost and yet another Grand Slam opportunity slipped away. The newspapers were ruthless in their assessment although, knowing the progress we were making, I found it hard to believe that some experts were calling for Clive to be sacked. To their credit, the RFU decision-makers weathered the storm and stayed calm, but our Grand Slam tribulations were not yet over.

The 2001 Six Nations decider between Ireland and England at Lansdowne Road was postponed for six months because of the outbreak of foot-and-mouth disease, and it did feel strange to be travelling to Dublin in the third week of October. Clive probably didn't have any option but to select the same players who had combined to win our first four matches in the championship, but several players' form had dipped and the team seemed to have lost impetus.

Ireland were all over us from the start and, while we certainly didn't lack desire, we just couldn't click into gear and function as a unit. Having started on the bench, I got a run when Daws pulled his hamstring after around half an hour. Yet, within five minutes, Keith Wood tackled me heavily, popping out my ribs and, with nobody left to cover on the bench, I had to play on. The match became a mad, green blur and, once again, we were defeated.

Lightning had struck three times. Why? How? I don't know. All three defeats were away from home. Each time, the opposition had been on fire and we were off form, but, each time, to be honest, we hadn't really deserved to win. Ultimately, that's sport. We had lost, and we had to take the knocks on the chin.

The management correctly tried to keep things positive and in perspective, pointing out that, in 2000 and 2001, we had still won the Six Nations. What we had lost was the Grand Slam, the 100 per cent record. They were right, of course, but the logic didn't provide much consolation to us or the coach. What we wanted, what Clive wanted, was the World Cup, and, if we were going to be good enough to win the World Cup, we needed to win Grand Slams.

At last, things have come together in 2003, this year. We won the Grand Slam, and followed that up with the summer wins over New Zealand and Australia. We have now beaten South Africa in the big group match of this World Cup, and overcome the French in the semi-final. Perhaps everything is falling into place when it matters most. I hope so. We'll find out in Sydney tonight.

Clive is still enjoying his breakfast, but he has stopped eating and now seems to be involved in an intense, animated discussion with his assistants. He's clearly relishing the debate. Many people in positions of authority seem scared of gathering talented people around them, preferring to be surrounded by fools who make them look good. Not Clive: he has assembled almost certainly the finest, most qualified management team in rugby history.

Every individual is a recognised expert in his field,

respected by Clive and, crucially, respected by the players. They may also be one of the largest management teams in rugby history, and I won't be surprised if they are the most highly paid, but the players share the coach's view that the quality of this support is crucial if we are to achieve that 'extra 1 per cent' of performance.

Since Clive himself was a back-line player, his assistant coach has always worked with the forwards. His initial selection was John Mitchell, a respected player and coach, who he lured from Sale to turn the pack into a ruthless unit. When John stepped down in 2000, Clive turned to Andy Robinson, who was also highly respected, and the forwards have continued to prosper.

Perhaps Clive's most important appointment was that of Phil Larder as the defensive coach. Nobody in English rugby union had traditionally worried much about defence in the past. It was either 'man-on', which meant you tackled the opponent in front of you, or it was 'slide', which meant you tackled the man one along, and that was that. Everything was focused on attack.

Clive had travelled to the United States and spent some time watching American gridiron training. Those squads are divided into three – an offensive team, a defensive team and a special team – and he returned home resolved that we should spend the same amount of time on our defence as we spend on our attack.

Some of the guys were initially sceptical, but Phil's passion for this element of the game won everyone over. He made us feel as if defence was more important than anything. Just look at the last two Rugby World Cups, he told us. South Africa won in 1995, primarily because they conceded the fewest tries, and Australia did the same when they took the Webb Ellis Cup four years later. In major team events, the best defence usually comes out on top.

It all makes sense, and Phil gets stuck into us. He shouts and roars the whole time, nit-picking every detail, constantly striving for perfection. Defensive patterns have been created and are rehearsed until every member of the squad knows exactly where they must be and what they must do in every imaginable situation.

Phil is a demanding taskmaster, which is good, and those of us with long memories know he can also be pretty ruthless. Back in 1997, before we played the All Blacks at Old Trafford, Phil got a bee in his bonnet that Ade Adebayo, our winger, didn't communicate to the forwards about helping out in defence. Ade didn't have a great game, mainly because his confidence had been shot to pieces, and at one stage he didn't hear a back-line call and was caught seriously out of position. At the post-match team meeting, Phil proceeded to criticise Ade so much that, even today, several of us are careful of what we say around him. He's fantastic at his job, but he has Clive's ear and he's not a good man to upset.

The irony of that situation in 1997 is that Ade probably knew the calls better than most of the guys. Lawrence Dallaglio was one of many who didn't have everything clear in his head and, early in the Test against the All Blacks, as I prepared to put the ball into a scrum I shouted out the call 'rhino', which meant Lol was supposed to collect the ball at the back and carry it upfield. Next, all I could hear was the muffled sound of Lol's voice deep inside our scrum, pleading: 'What the **** does "rhino" mean?' I had just enough time to tell him, and nobody noticed, not even Phil.

Another key member of Clive's crew is Dave Alred, the kicking coach, a man with a diverse background that includes playing rugby union for Bristol, earning a living as a kicker in the American NFL and being involved in Australian Rules. The result is that, although he doesn't kick with both feet, I would say he is undoubtedly the best kicker of a rugby ball that I have ever seen. When your coach is that good, it's very easy to listen and learn.

His expertise has added many aspects to our game, perhaps most notably the cross-kick that Jonny places behind the opposition defence for our wing to run through and collect. Executed correctly, it is almost impossible to defend. One word of warning: Dave spent some time with the Wallabies as well, and the cross-kick is usually part of their armoury too. We'll have to be careful tonight.

Dave has also ventured into the field of psychology, showing the squad how keeping folders full of information and motivational tools can help our preparation for a Test. He is also extremely keen on visualisation as mental preparation. Citing Tiger Woods' habit of imagining the perfect flight of every shot before he swings the club, he says we can use the same technique in rugby. He's bright, keen, enthusiastic and a great person to have around.

There are other essential members of the team: Simon Hardy is our line-out specialist and works tirelessly with the throwers and jumpers to make sure England win not only all our own line-outs, but also a healthy chunk of opposition ball. Line-outs are a crucial phase; the days of throw and hope are long gone. Phil Keith-Roach, our scrum specialist, is a major reason why we have been so strong in this area over the past few years. Bossing the scrum is fundamental in our overall plan to dominate the game.

Clive has also handpicked the best available nutritionalists, chefs, physiotherapists, doctors, masseurs, media officers, hand-eye and vision trainers and fitness instructors. We even have the team QC, to deal with any legal problems that may arise. I think it's accurate to say that, in constructing his team behind the team, the coach has thought of just about everything. He presides over the entire structure, giving his experts the freedom to operate in their own fields, but always keeping watch. If anything goes wrong in a specific area, he demands an explanation and a solution from the responsible coach. The system isn't rocket science, but it's rigorous and clear, and it works.

I look across and see the coach is leaving the dining room with his assistants. He seems relaxed and confident. That's perfect. Everybody picks up on his mood, and it's important that he feels positive. He's done a fantastic job for England. Win or lose tonight, Clive Woodward is easily the best coach I have known.

CHAPTER FOUR

9.46 a.m.
Saturday, 22 November 2003
ENGLAND TEAM HOTEL, SYDNEY

It's pandemonium in the hotel foyer. There are security guards at the front door who are meant to restrict entry to hotel guests, but it now seems as if the entire West Stand at Twickenham has managed to find a way in, and they all want autographs.

It's great, but it's getting too much. Everybody is excited, and everybody is chattering, but we're counting down the hours to the biggest match of our lives and we don't want chaos. Every time a player emerges from the lift bleary-eyed on his way to breakfast, he gets a huge cheer. These supporters mean well, but right now we need a bit of peace and quiet.

I am standing to one side, keeping my head down, watching the scene, and I can see Clive is starting to get concerned. It seems some of the guys had been trying to have breakfast but people kept approaching them, asking for photos and signatures. Today of all days, we should have got a private dining room. It's ridiculous that we have to eat with so many people around.

The hullabaloo is too much, so I go back to my room, lie down on the bed and close my eyes. All I can hear are the distant cheers of about a thousand England supporters now standing in the street outside the front entrance of the hotel. They're chanting for players to give them a wave from the window of their rooms, and they roar with delight every time one of them obliges.

I hope I get on. I really hope I get on. I've been a substitute on the England bench so many times over the past decade, but I've never really got used to the feeling. This is going to be the biggest match of my career, and I can't bear to think that I may not even get a run, may not even get my knees dirty.

It's weird. Right now, there is nothing I want so much as for England to beat Australia tonight and win the World Cup. It's what we have been working towards for so long. It means everything to us. And yet that's not the whole story, because I really want to get a run and the competitive side of me wants a few things to go wrong, so they will have to make changes and give me a chance.

Some time ago, Clive introduced a code of conduct where, as soon as the Test team is announced, if you're not included you are supposed to approach the guy picked ahead of you, shake him by the hand and offer your congratulations. I have done my fair share of hand shaking over the years but, earlier this week, when I was shaking Daws by the hand, it felt strange.

On the outside I was smiling, patting him on the back and wishing him all the best, but on the inside I found myself hoping he has a real shocker, so they'll bring me on. That's how it is. I don't feel guilty about it. It's not personal. It's just that I am competitive. I desperately want to play for England in the World Cup final, and if he has to fail to make that happen, so be it.

Daws may as well be two completely different people so far as I'm concerned. On the one hand, he's a nice guy and a good friend who has worked unbelievably hard to get where he is today. I really like him and genuinely wish him all the best. On the other hand, he has become the barrier between me and my dream.

In fact, this week we have spent time together helping each other prepare, talking about the game, discussing the best way to play the Australian scrum-half, George Gregan, and we have worked well together, sharing knowledge and experience. Gregan is a great player but, like anyone else, he has his weaknesses. Daws and I agree he's open to being caught at the base of the scrum, and we reckon he can be quite fiery, so there's a chance he'll lose his temper if he gets held on the ground for a few extra seconds after being tackled. We mentioned that in a team meeting, and the forwards will push him down.

The day is dragging on, as I knew it would. It's barely ten in the morning and there are still eight hours before we leave for the stadium. I hope I get on. My parents should be awake by now. I decide to go and see them, and arrive to find them looking happy and relaxed, taking their time over a champagne breakfast. Just as it's a massive day for me, so it's a massive day for them as well.

Dad asks if I want a game of chess and, for a moment, I reckon he might go easy on me, maybe even let me win just to give me a boost. No chance. He wins, as usual, but we laugh, and I relax and really enjoy spending time with my mum and dad. When my brother John and my sister Jane arrive in the room the family banter soon starts and all the pressure and tension of the day seems to melt away. I'm just plain old Kyran again. Nobody is questioning me, nobody is studying me, nobody is judging me, nobody is doubting me, nobody is asking if my back is OK, nobody wants a photo or an autograph. I'm just me.

After an hour or so, I make my way down to the team room, where most of the guys are watching a film on the video. This is our space, and everyone looks relaxed. There's the normal chirping. A few of the guys are sitting apart, alone, studying their match folder, checking, running through moves in their heads. I'm feeling OK, no problems, no real nerves yet. I just hope I get on.

Lunch is light, a sandwich and one of my chocolate brownies saved from the day before. It has become a tradition in the England squad that, on the eve of every international match, our chef makes a load of his renowned chocolate brownies and puts them in the team room at exactly four o'clock. He did that before a Test against Australia a couple of years ago, we won and, by popular demand, he has been doing it ever since. There is always a mad scramble to get them and the tray is emptied in seconds, but they taste great and, as I savour one for my lunch, I catch a couple of the others looking enviously in my direction. I smile. It's sad, but true.

At last the day is starting to gather momentum and, early afternoon, everyone gathers for a team meeting. I look around at all the faces. It's happening. Part of me always doubted whether we would reach this time and place, but here we are, running through our final preparations for the World Cup final. We've come so far as a team; now there's just one more step to make.

Clive opens the meeting, looking efficient and business-like, and asks if everyone is feeling OK. There have been times over the years when someone has woken on match day feeling terrible and had to withdraw, but this was not a day when anybody was going to tell the coach that, actually, they have a bit of headache and they're not feeling that great and they'll sit this one out. Everybody is fine; Daws looks so fit and eager. I hope I get a run.

The coach says his piece, urging us to stay relaxed and take things easy. Several of the coaches add a few words and, as usual, Phil Larder makes the biggest impression. I remember he once told us how a rugby league World Cup final had been decided by a single missed tackle. Each of us wants to make sure we're not the one who makes a crucial mistake tonight.

As I listen, I find myself wondering whether his dentures are going to fall out. Some of the guys give Phil a hard time when he struggles with his false teeth – I suppose the originals are buried on some rugby league field in the north of England – and he starts to lisp or whistle through his words, but he finishes intact. The fact is we all have massive respect for Phil Larder. He has developed and communicated a world-class defensive system, which we all know has been a major reason for our recent success.

Not much is said about our tactics for the final, because most of the work has been covered earlier in the week and each of us has spent so much time with our heads in our folders that we all know the strategies and moves by heart. Do I? I think so, but, to make absolutely sure, I repeat everything in my mind . . .

Traits of Australia: back three like to attack with a lot of width, using cross-field kicks for wingers; will try and exploit a short side if we overcommit on far side; will keep hold of ball for long periods and will try to tire us out; have scored lots of tries through turnovers because they are quick to see when scoring opportunity is on; will attack from kick-offs from deep; rely on Waugh and Smith to run the rucks and mauls; able to dominate possession, with more than 60 per cent in last few games; started to use quick taps to speed up the game; Lyons is the only forward to be a ball carrier, so will use backs Tuqiri, Sailor, Mortlock and Flatley to carry the ball; Gregan and Larkham like to boss the game. Gregan carries ball to line and runs across field searching for holes, using inside flip ball very well. Larkham carries ball with pace, runs an outside arc well and uses the inside ball if nothing is on; will use inside switch ball to test our inside defence; use decoy runners who obstruct.

Is there anything else? I don't think so.

England defence: always clear out 6, 7 and 8; at breakdown point, make the correct decision either to go in and slow down the ball or stay out and defend around the ruck; when tackling, stay low and drive through their legs; don't get hand-offs from big runners; second man in targets the ball; control the middle of the pitch and crowd Gregan, so he can't run across the field; stay aware of inside runners; inside defence must stay together and communicate to get spacing between each other right; run fast at Larkham, forcing him to make early decisions; deny them momentum at first phase; kick forward and chase together, leaving three back, including one back-row forward. Key words: patience; work-rate; desire.

I'm feeling like an actor waiting for the curtain to rise on the biggest night of his career, when millions and millions of people will be watching every move. I have to know this stuff.

England attack: go forward with multiphase attack; dominate the contact area; hit 6 and 7 off the ball before the ruck starts; ball carriers must drive with their legs; use pick-and-go option to move the ball away from contact as soon as possible; use direct running out wide; use decoys against their slide defence; attack their front five with drives; focus on Larkham and Smith as poor defenders; kick behind their wingers for our wingers to catch; defensive kicks must reach the seats in the stands to prevent quick line-outs; never kick into open field and invite their back three to counter; play with pace at scrum and line-out; increase tempo with free kicks and penalties; only slow down the game when instructed by Johnno; keep penalties down to minimum; build the score by taking every opportunity to accumulate points in their half; be prepared to use the drop-goal routine if and when required.

That's the lot: Australia's patterns, our defence and attack. It all makes sense. We're focusing on their half-backs and their back three as the strengths, and their tight five as the weakness. We are happy with the strategy, and we understand it. Now it's a question of making sure everything is implemented correctly.

Most people believe this is Johnno's responsibility, but this is an England side that runs onto the field with eight or nine captains, each tasked to direct a different aspect of the game. Johnno is our leader, the man who gets us going, the strong beating heart of the team, the talisman, the icon who pulls us together when things get rough, but the nitty-gritty job of ensuring we play according to plan is shared by captains all over the field. Johnno can always overrule any player on anything but, once the game has started, the only decision that lies with him alone is whether or not we should kick for goal when we are awarded a penalty.

Phil Vickery is the captain of our scrum, and he is responsible for that mysterious, dark area of the game that anyone outside the front row doesn't even pretend to understand. When the props and hooker gather together with their specialist coach, Phil Keith-Roach, they get very serious and technical, which can be intimidating for a scrum-half, who is only invited to join the group because he has to put the ball into the scrum. They have spent many hours this week studying the Aussie scrum on video over and over again, and I know Phil and the front row are adamant we can dominate the final by targeting their scrum and tiring their tight five.

Earlier this year, before a Test when I was in the starting side, I was told to attend one of these front-row meetings, and it turned out to be a real eye-opener. They started by ordering enough room service for an entire team and eventually settled down with either a pot of tea each or a chilled bottle of beer. They then proceeded to watch scrum after scrum on video, discussing binding, feet position, everything you can imagine. After two hours of this, I was stuffed full of tea and cake, and bored out of my mind. Oddly, I haven't ever been invited back into this inner sanctum.

I have still learned all their calls as well, so I know what to do when Vickers calls for a *wheel left*, or a *wheel right*, or a *push right through*, or a *wait for push once ball is in*, or a *step across the mark and shuffle right*, or a *step across the mark and shuffle left*, or a *take it all down if not happy*, or *bore in on their hooker on their ball*, or *squeeze at the same time*, or many other variations.

Ben Kay has been appointed to direct the line-outs, making all the calls and taking the rap if anything goes wrong. He knows what he is doing, but I am concerned that we have over-complicated and have too many calls and too many options. It's one thing for the guys to have everything under control with plenty of time and little opposition on the training field, but the calls can very quickly get muddled and confused in the heat of the battle. The Australians are nimble at the line-out, and we'll need to be careful.

Phil Larder works closely with two special defensive captains, Neil Back among the forwards and Will Greenwood in the back line, and these two always take leading roles whenever we practise our defensive formations. This week they have successfully persuaded Phil to go easy on the training, but we have still spent a lot of time discussing every possible scenario, dreaming up ways the Aussies may try to penetrate, and planning our response. Such is his relentless passion, Phil is endlessly asking what if this, what if that, and it's usually Backy who tells him to chill out; and Phil actually listens. In fact, the pair of them seem to get along and understand each other so well that the guys have begun to refer to Backy as 'Phil's lost son' or 'Phil's mini-me'.

The scrum-half is put in charge of the contact area, as well as deciding the direction of our kick-offs and 22-metre dropouts. Since we can drop back and are best placed to see where the opposition is standing, we operate as the eyes of the team. We also work in conjunction with Jonny to determine the overall pattern of play, assessing every specific situation during the game and making a snap decision whether to break, pass or kick.

This is a massive responsibility, and it probably explains why the half-backs are usually the fall guys if things go wrong. When the game goes well, people say it's because the pack is 'dominating' or the backs are 'taking their chances'. But if things go badly, none of those guys cop the flack because, more often than not, they say it was the half-backs who 'took the wrong options'.

It is the wingers who make the calls when we receive restarts, deciding how we move back upfield, and it will be Jonny and Mike Tindall who run the kicking strategy, determining when and where we kick. Clive is adamant that whenever we kick into touch we must kick the ball right into the crowd, and he goes ballistic if we don't do that and the opposition takes a quick line-out. That's good coaching; everyone knows exactly what he wants.

Of course, Clive has some previous form in this particular area of the game. Third Test, South Africa v Lions, 1980, Boet Erasmus Stadium in Port Elizabeth, pouring rain: trailing 2–0 in the four-Test series, Bill Beaumont's Lions are clinging to a narrow lead with a few minutes left, keeping the rubber alive. The South Africans kick into the corner and the Lions wing only nudges the ball into touch, when he should have thumped it into Row Z. The Springboks take a quick throw-in, charge over to score in the corner and Naas Botha kicks the touchline conversion to win the match and the series. The name of that Lions winger was ... Clive Woodward. No wonder the idea of history repeating itself drives him mad.

Time moves on, and I go with the forwards to practise a few line-outs in a local park. Maybe my fears are misplaced. Our hooker, Steve Thompson, is hitting the jumpers and everything appears to be running smoothly as we go through the calls. When we arrive back at the hotel, we run a gauntlet of cheering supporters. Everyone is getting worked up. You can feel it. It's almost four o'clock now, just four hours until kick-off. I hope I get a run.

Most of the guys are hanging around the team room. Nobody wants to be alone in their rooms, because the adrenaline is starting to flow and you just want to get involved and feel the buzz. Is that clock on the wall working? Is it only half past?

Even the 'driftwood' are there, those guys in the tour party who have not been included in the twenty-two-man squad. They wear suits on match days and generally feel left out. It's not much fun being 'drift' on a normal tour, but at least you get to play in the midweek matches; it's even worse in the knockout stages of a World Cup, because the first XV always plays and there are no other matches, so these players are basically training with no prospect of getting a run unless somebody gets injured.

Clive has tried to keep the drift involved. Right at the start of the campaign, he said he didn't want any 'energisers, sappers or parasites' getting in the way of the team and the goal of winning the World Cup, and he hates to hear of anybody moaning or walking round with long faces. It's not so easy. You're talking about people who have just missed out on being involved in what would have been the biggest match of their lives, and Clive expects them to be as upbeat and cheerful as Butlin's redcoats.

In fairness, the drift have responded. They have all got stuck in at the practice sessions and worked hard to help the team. We're all aware of their contribution, and Johnno often goes out of his way to thank them for their efforts, making the drift out to be the real unsung heroes of our World Cup campaign.

We have been told to put our kitbags on the bus before the last team meeting starts at six o'clock, which doesn't seem a great idea because it means we have to negotiate the crowds at the front of the hotel once again, but the supporters won't complain, because it gives them another glimpse of the players. Everyone gets a cheer as they hurry out to the bus, drop their bag and scamper back to the refuge of the team room but, just as I get back inside the foyer, there is an amazing, deafening roar. What on earth was that? It was Jonny putting his bag on the bus.

As our final meeting starts, the nerves suddenly rise to the surface. The guys are quiet. Clive looks hyper, eyes darting this way and that, fretting, worrying about everything in general and nothing in particular. He gets up to speak, and wisely keeps it short. There's not much to be said now. 'Keep your heads,' he tells us. 'Enjoy the day. Come on, boys, let's win this thing.'

We pace straight out of the team room, down to the foyer and onto the bus. It's happening. There's no turning back now. Everyone is looking straight ahead, trying to avoid eye contact with anyone else, each in their own world, dealing with their own pressure, coping, getting ready. I hope I get on.

It's a forty-five-minute bus journey to the Telstra Stadium, formerly known as Stadium Australia, the main venue of the Olympic Games in 2000, and, although we get a police escort to the highway, most of us are soon gazing out of the window at people tooting their horns and waving as they drive up alongside us. Most of them appear to be Australian because, to judge from the hand signals, they don't seem to be wishing us the best of luck. Some of the guys think it's quite funny, and the sound of laughter eases the tension.

Clive has put in a CD compilation that his daughter, Jess, has apparently put together, and he turns up the volume. It's mostly dance music with a really heavy beat and, as it throbs through the speakers, filling the bus with relentless rhythm, Lol excitedly stands up and starts bouncing around in the aisle.

Sitting near the front of the bus, I turn to look back and see Johnno sitting still with his eyes shut. That's amazing, I thought to myself. He's on his way to this huge occasion and his confidence is such that he thinks he can actually fall asleep. The captain has got his usual bottle of yellow carbs on his lap, while the rest of us sip on the mineral water and Lucozade provided.

Daws is listening to his own music through a massive pair of headphones. Jonny looks as white as a sheet, as though he might throw up at any moment. He always gets sullen and serious before a big game, and he usually dreads the build-up, mainly because he puts so much pressure on himself to perform. It's nothing to worry about. He's OK. It's his way of getting ready.

We're not far away now. Clive keeps turning around, peering back down the aisle, checking his players. He sees Johnno with his eyes shut, and I know the coach hates the idea of anyone falling asleep on the bus, but he doesn't say anything. He's really getting into the music, tapping out the beat on his knee. In fact, he looks as if he's about ready to run out and play himself.

The weather has been overcast all day, but it is starting to rain heavily. So much for the hot-weather training, I mumble to Catty as the bus pulls up outside the stadium. The conditions are not really an issue for us. Wet or dry, we're ready.

Clive gets to his feet beside the driver and, as usual when we arrive at the stadium before an international, he stands there and takes care to shake the hand of every player as we file past out of the bus, into the stadium and off towards the changing room. 'Be ready, KB,' he tells me. I am. I hope I get on.

Our kit man, Dave Tennison, is nicknamed Reg, after the character in *The Bill*, because he organises everything with military precision. He has come from the Royal Marines, and as we walk in it is immediately clear that he has outdone himself in preparing our changing room. Our playing kit is ironed, neatly folded and laid out in each place. St George flags have been draped above every seat, and there are even larger flags hung on the walls with mottos written on them, like *We're here to win* and *This is England*. I look around and find myself getting a lump in my throat. Relax, Kyran, calm down. It's only the World Cup final.

Jonny immediately starts getting changed, as if he can't wait to get immersed in the security and familiarity of his usual warm-up routine, but the rest of us are happy to take our time. Some of the guys sit and page through the programme, while others, including me, take a walk out to get a feel of the stadium as the spectators start to arrive. It's still raining quite heavily.

The atmosphere is electric, unlike anything I have ever known or will know. You see it on every face and hear it in every word. As much as we want to prepare as though this is just another game, it isn't just another game. To a large extent, the events of the next two hours are going to define the rest of our lives. Will we go down in English sporting history as champions, or chokers?

Such thoughts quicken my heartbeat. I feel it. Calm down,

I tell myself again, keep control. I have a habit of doing stupid things when I'm under pressure. Before a big league match last season, I ran out without putting on shoulder pads. Concentrate. Don't make a mistake. I get changed into my playing kit, and check everything once, then again, and then for a third time.

My back is feeling fine but, just for insurance, I walk to the physio's area and get myself a soothing lower-back massage with good old Deep Heat. I love that stuff, getting burning hot and ready for action, although it can hurt if you let any of the cream get on the more sensitive parts of your body. Jason Leonard and I are just about the only remaining members of the squad who still use rugby's time-honoured warm-up. We're from the old school and we take great delight in stinking out the whole changing room. If it was good enough in the 1960s, it's good enough now.

I'm glad to get my rub finished early, so I don't get in the way of the guys in the starting XV. I go back to my place in the changing room and begin strapping my ankles. It's the most boring part of the prematch routine but it has to be done and as I start wrapping the bandage, taking care not to strain my back, I look around at the guys getting ready, just taking in the scene.

The front row are all together, as usual. They always seem to take an age to get changed, wandering around in nothing but their undies with their guts hanging out. They're mumbling in their own language, talking about what boots they're going to wear in the wet conditions. I reckon they'll go for the long studs and wonder if they will first go through one of rugby's charming charades.

Before every match, it is the referee's job to visit each of the teams in their changing room and check their studs. I have often seen front rows show the ref their boots and everything seems fine but, as soon as the official has gone, they each take out a second pair, with much longer studs, and change into them. It happens so frequently I'm sure the referees must know exactly what's going on, but they just choose to turn a blind eye.

André Watson, the South African referee appointed to handle tonight's game, arrives in our changing room on cue, and solemnly inspects the boots of the props and hooker. He then tells them how he wants to see space between the front rows before they engage, and Vicks chats to him, clarifying a few points.

Johnno is taking his time, methodically strapping each of his fingers, one after the other, both hands. I assume it helps him catch the ball. Maybe I should try it some time. His body bears the scars of so many operations, and he looks such a warrior. Thank goodness he's on our side.

I glance across at Will Greenwood and notice he's wearing his lucky T-shirt underneath his jersey. It's a skanky thing these days, with holes and a picture printed on the front, but it makes him feel good. I've never been particularly superstitious, but many of the guys do or wear something that helps them to settle down. Jason Robinson generally seems to like walking around the changing room without his jersey on. I watch him stroll past. That guy is an unbelievable ball of pure muscle.

Backy's routine is to empty the entire contents of his kitbag on the changing room floor, as if he has just arrived at army camp, and then to fold everything away in perfectly lined-up piles. There have been several occasions when I have amused myself by nipping over and messing up his impeccable stacks, but I'm not going to do that today. Lol and Hilly are just standing around. Maybe they're waiting for him, so the back row can warm up together.

The changing room is quiet. Everybody is nervous, rightly, but the mood is good. Nobody's panicking. I spend a few minutes on a vibrating machine, which is a kind of platform that shakes your entire body while you do your stretches and is meant to get you really well warmed up. To be honest, it doesn't do much for me, but Ben Kay says it helps him with his knee. Anyway, it won't do me any harm and there's nothing else to do. Time is beginning to drag again. It's not long now. I hope I get on.

Most of the backs are ready, so I join a group that goes out to practise some kicking and passing on the field. It's still raining, but not as heavily as before. The stadium appears about 60 per cent full, and there are St George flags all over the place. 'Is this Sydney or Twickenham?' jokes one of the guys. I'm astonished. The sheer scale of our support so far from home is unbelievable. I put in a few long strides and throw a few passes, just to get a feel of the ball. Daws does his normal thing, some goal-kicking practice followed by a few changes of direction. He's looking sharp.

There are now just twenty-five minutes until kick-off, and we're called together for one last team meeting. Andy Robinson talks. 'Pressure! Work-rate! Build the score! Physicality!' he says. Robbo and I have had our differences over the years. There's nothing unusual in that. That happens in any sport. But he's been as much a part of this as anyone else. Now, his message is clear and concise.

Phil Larder adds a few words. Lol is getting fired up. In fact, pretty soon everyone is breathing fire, motivating each other. This kind of thing comes naturally to most of the England guys because when we play for our clubs we're all used to playing an active role in psyching up the team. We're all leaders. 'Let's ******* get into them,' Vicks shouts, exactly as he would if he was back home at Gloucester. 'This is it, boys,' Lol bellows, as he does before Wasps take the field. 'No hiding.' Backy is charged. 'Let's tear into them,' he barks, as he would at Leicester. We're together.

Johnno isn't saying too much, but most of us instinctively look towards him at moments like this. He stands bolt upright, pumped full of power and emotion, looking as if he's about to burst, and he starts to lead us out for a warm-up on the pitch. We march slowly in single file and only explode into a sprint, one after the other, when we feel the grass beneath our studs. The stadium erupts. We charge straight into the noise, straight into the occasion. I love this moment. All the pent-up energies and nerves are released and you run, suddenly feeling like a fearless eighteen-year-old, unbeatable. All the old aches and pains seem to melt away.

We form a circle, arms bound around each other's shoulders, twenty-two hearts going crazy, and our captain goes berserk. '******* come on,' Johnno shouts. 'Feel it! Look around! This is ******* it! We're going to shut their crowd up and climb into them!' Bits of spit are flying out of his mouth. This is Johnno at his most aggressive. He's on fire, and every single one of us is right there with him, listening to every word. I feel so strong. I hope I get on.

The guys go through the usual warm-up routine and then go back inside for the final bit of preparations, and the last opportunity to get rid of the last drop in the toilet. It's amazing what nerves do to your bowels. Guys are breaking wind all over the place, some get diarrhoea and the place is soon smelling like a sewer. Daws takes his scribbled notes with him into the cubicle, pins them to the wall and has one last check while he's on the loo. As he comes back into the changing room, I wish him luck. I mean it.

Jonny still looks ashen-faced, and the forwards are starting to pace up and down, eager to rip into contact. Johnno is calmer now, more like the dominant alpha male overseeing his pack, his strong men. Perhaps he regards the backs as his harem of females. The forwards would like to think so. The captain calls the starting team into a huddle and that's the sign for us, the substitutes, to leave the changing room. It's an England tradition that the subs get into two lines outside and cheer the guys onto the field.

Come on, Johnno, I shout as they come thundering past. Come on, Daws. We follow on after the last man and, by the time the stadium turns yellow as the Australians emerge, we're into another huddle. '******* awesome!' Johnno yells. 'Soak it in, boys. Let's get stuck into them.'

The anthems start. Will Greenwood looks as if he's just seen a ghost. He's had to deal with a lot over the past few weeks, having had to fly home for a few days to help his pregnant wife though an anxious time, but everything is settled now and he's come through it all. It was a major thing for the squad to lose a key guy in the middle of the tournament but, in a way, Will's situation helped us all to keep the rugby in some kind of perspective. This is a World Cup final, this is huge, but it's still not everything.

' . . . God save the Queen!' We may not be the choir at St Paul's, and some of the guys seem to shout the words rather than sing, but, whatever else is true, the England rugby team certainly don't lack passion during our national anthem. In some ways, it's our haka. It means a lot to us, never more so than tonight.

I take my place on the bench, beside Jason Leonard, and just as the 2003 World Cup final kicks off, I feel a splash of warm liquid on my right sock. Fantastic! Jase is pissing on me. Hidden from view by the tackle bag in front of us, he's adjusted himself out of the side of his shorts and a donkey stream of pee is splattering over my sock and boots. I protest. He thinks it's hilarious.

The match becomes a blur of contact and movement, English white against Australian gold. The line-outs are not going well, and the Wallabies steal one of our moves when Tuqiri scores a try after catching a cross-kick, but we're doing OK. My whole body seems to brace whenever I see Daws disappear under a ruck or a maul, thinking he could be injured and I might suddenly get the call; then I ease back as he emerges, on his feet, still strong.

Sitting in the front row of the stand behind us, all dressed in their grey suits, the drift are sniggering, laughing at each other, having a wonderful time. It seems that Joe Worsley has bought a large bottle of vodka and a load of Red Bulls, and mixed them all together in the official England team water bottles. Not a bad idea, I thought. Hey presto, the driftwood are flying.

I get a sense that the game is much closer than it should be. We are basically running the match but we haven't moved ahead, for two reasons. One, our line-outs are a shambles. People are beginning to blame Thommo for his throwing, but it's not all his fault. The problem is a combination of that, bad lifting and predictable options. Second, André Watson is repeatedly penalising us in the scrums, which seems crazy, because we generally seem to get the shove on them.

Daws is having a decent game, and he breaks on the blind

side, creating a two-on-one situation. It seems we must score, but Ben Kay spills a pass with the line at his mercy. Never mind. Stay calm. We eventually do get a try when Lol storms through a gap on the open side, puts Jonny away and he feeds Jason Robinson, who races over in the corner. It means so much to him. He punches the ball away and screams 'Come on!' at the crowd.

Every fifteen minutes or so, we jog down the side of the pitch and do some exercises in the area behind the posts. Subs are meant to keep warm and always be ready. As we stretch, the supporters in the stand are brilliant, shouting out our names. They're getting a bit anxious, and so are we. We should have the game won, but the Wallabies keep clawing their way back. Elton Flatley is nailing huge pressure kick after huge pressure kick. Surely we can't throw this away. I'm a bag of nerves. Watching is terrible. The scores are level at 14–14 when Watson blows the final whistle of normal time.

We run on the field to help prepare for extra time. Daws must be knackered. Surely I'm going to get a run now. I'm involved, but I want to get on the park and feel part of it. I keep looking at Clive, hoping to get a sign. He doesn't look at me. He is telling the guys to be patient. Robbo has got his Filofax out, trying to sort out the problems we're still having in the line-out.

Johnno is calm and firm. He politely asks the coaches to leave the players alone, and then tells us to maintain the work-rate, stay as patient as possible and take the chance when it comes. We're all listening, except Jonny. I notice he's gone off to the opposite end of the pitch and is practising his place kicks and drop goals. That guy is so focused. If anyone deserves success, it's him.

There's still no nod from Clive. As I wander back to the bench, a thought strikes me. If the scores are still level at the end of extra time, the rules stipulate that the World Cup final will be decided by a drop-goal competition. What will happen then? Who will take the kicks, and in what order? Nobody has mentioned the subject. Clive hasn't said a word about it at any meeting. Maybe he has a plan up his sleeve. I don't know. I hope so. What happens if I'm on the field at the end? I've never been that good at drop goals.

Still the contest is tight. Clive comes down from his seat in the stand towards the end, as he usually does, and sits with us on the bench. I look at him. Please get me on. I just want to be able to say I did my bit. Even if it's only for ten seconds, I just want to play in a World Cup final, to feel involved in everything.

He watches the game. We all watch. Seconds are left. We're seconds away from the great unknown of the drop-goal shoot-out. Daws makes a break, then Johnno takes the ball into a ruck. We get the ball back – and Jonny slots the drop goal with his right foot. Everybody is on their feet. The England fans are going crazy. Jonny is amazing. Confronted by one chance to win the game, he goes with what is supposedly his weaker foot, but that's the whole point about him: I've watched him in training and he simply does not have a weaker foot.

It's almost done. The Wallabies restart. I look at Clive one last time. Please, please get me on. Look at me and see the pleading in my eyes. He doesn't. He's watching the match. It's not going to happen. There is virtually no time left. Catty punts the ball into the stands, and suddenly it's all over. Bedlam breaks out. We have won the World Cup. We've done what England expected. We've realised our full potential and fulfilled our greatest dream.

I find myself feeling absolutely thrilled ... and devastated at the same time. I so much wanted to be able to grow old and look back and say I played in a World Cup final. I've come so far and got just about as close as it's possible to get, but I haven't actually played in what still ranks as the biggest match of my life. Maybe I'm wrong. I have been involved. I've been in and around this squad for the past ten years. My part was my performance in the match against South Africa, wasn't it? I did my bit, I hope. I'm confused.

As the Aussies go up to collect their runners-up medals, we're just standing around, grinning, hugging each other, laughing, simply enjoying every second of the victory rites. It is finally our turn to climb onto the podium and receive our medals from John Howard, the Australian Prime Minister. It can't be much fun for him, but he seems like a decent guy. We want to keep moving.

Johnno gets hold of the cup, and he raises it aloft in a burst of flashbulbs, creating the image that will be engraved in the mind of every England rugby supporter for generations to come. I stare into the stand, looking for my family, and spot them. John is grinning. Mum and Dad look happy. They'll see the big picture and be proud I have been involved in something so special. I hope my sister Jane doesn't think hers has been a wasted trip, flying around the world to watch her brother sit on the bench. I am missing Victoria terribly. Most of the guys are blowing kisses at their wives and girlfriends in the stand, and I wish my wife could be here.

We stroll around the lap of honour, stopping now and then for the joyful, bouncing, chanting kind of squad photograph that seems to have become the norm at every big final. I get my hands on the Webb Ellis trophy. It feels fantastic and, in that instant, most of the disappointment of not getting on seems to drain away. I have been part of this. So has Simon Shaw, and he hasn't had a chance to get on the field in the entire tournament. We have planned as a squad, trained as a squad and we have won as a squad.

The celebrations continue back in our changing room. Various dignitaries arrive, with Prince Harry and John Howard coming in to offer their congratulations. Some of the guys produce the expensive cameras they bought in Singapore on the way over, and everyone is posing for everyone else. I'm snapping away with the best of them and get a superb picture of Hilly standing in the shower with all his kit on, holding a beer, smiling like a champion.

Clive stands apart, and isn't bothered about getting into any photos with the cup. He has pursued this thing for so long. Judge me on the World Cup, he has told everyone throughout his coaching career, and now he has delivered. He's done it. That's enough, and he feels no urge to dominate the pictures.

It is past midnight by the time everyone is back on the bus, and we head off towards a press conference. The journalists swarm over the starting XV, which is to be expected, but for those of us standing quietly to one side, feeling a bit like spare parts, it's good to hear Johnno make a special point of saying the victory was won by the thirty-one-man squad, not just the fifteen.

When the last question has been answered, we all get back on the bus and move on to a place overlooking the Sydney Opera House, where we are reunited with our families. My parents, John and Jane look really excited and, although we are all thinking of my little sister, Louise, we have a great time, with everybody trying on my winner's medal. I apologise to Jane for not getting on the field, but she says she wouldn't have missed it for the world.

I haven't always been among the first to leave such occasions and I don't hesitate to have a few drinks and enjoy myself but, just after four in the morning, I decide I've had enough and join about half the guys on the team bus back to the hotel.

It isn't until everybody gathers for a debrief the following day that we hear the story of a group of lads who will forever be known as the Sydney Six. They had continued drinking through the night until they staggered out of a pub in the King's Cross area at about eleven on the Sunday morning. They were alarmed to be confronted by a police car, but quickly relieved when the policemen recognised who they were and offered them a lift.

The Sydney Six duly arrived back at our hotel. They climbed out of the back of the police van and, still very drunk, received a rapturous heroes' reception from several hundred supporters still standing outside the main entrance. Just then, a group of press photographers appeared on the scene and took photographs of the guys in the police van, but it was all taken in fun.

In the formal part of the debrief, Clive simply asks us to be patient with the razzmatazz that is inevitably going to surround us over the next few days. We are supposed to attend an official dinner that night, and nobody wants to go, but Clive leaves us in no doubt about our responsibilities and, with a few sore heads and some blurred vision, we know he is right.

Later that day, we all troop out to the beach to have some more photos taken with the cup. Somebody is on the ball because they produce a bundle of club jerseys, and we have a squad picture taken with each player wearing his club jersey. It's a neat gesture, because it recognises the massive role that our clubs, and the men who bankroll them, have played in the recent successes of rugby in England. When historians reflect on the 2003 World Cup, they must recognise the contribution of the club owners.

The dinner is as dull and predictable as we expected, and I can't wait to get home. There are people everywhere, asking for autographs and photos, and we want to oblige, but the crowds are suddenly all over us when we arrive at Sydney airport to catch our Monday evening flight to London. Jonny always seems to be the focus of everything, and he really doesn't enjoy it at all. He smiles, but he just doesn't want all this attention.

Daws is having a problem at the security gate. The bleeping sound goes off every time he walks through. He has emptied his pockets and isn't carrying anything and the guards can't understand what's wrong, until one of them notices Daws is wearing his World Cup winner's medal underneath his shirt.

After all the excitement and extended celebrations, everyone is exhausted by the time our plane touches down at Heathrow airport. 'Don't worry,' somebody says. 'It's five in the morning and, at most, there'll be a couple of hundred people there.' I don't disagree. After all, we're a bunch of rugby players, not pop stars.

The plane has been renamed 'Sweet Chariot' in our honour, and we have another squad photograph on the steps, bringing back memories of a similar picture on our departure. That was only two months ago, but so much has happened since, it almost feels as if two years has passed. That done, I look forward to strolling off to the bus and, before long, seeing Victoria again.

A couple of hundred people are making a hell of a lot of noise, the guys think, as we approach Arrivals at Terminal Four. I happen to walk through the gates beside Neil Back, who is holding the Webb Ellis trophy, and the place erupts. I get my camcorder out of my kitbag and start recording the mayhem. There is a sea of England fans, shouting and screaming at us, reaching out to touch us as we walk past. The place is packed.

It takes an age to walk the fifty metres to our bus. I finally sit down, completely gobsmacked. Bloody hell, I think, we must have done something special. We're heroes. I watch the guys arrive at the bus, one after the other, each smiling, eyes wide open, trying to take in what we've just seen and heard. Many of us have been in this squad for many years, through Grand Slams and Test wins, and none of us has ever known anything like this. We've entered a new world, so we may as well sit back and enjoy it.

The bus eventually moves off and when we at last arrive at the Pennyhill Park Hotel, I rush out and fall into the arms of my wife. I promise never to leave her for so long again. Her tummy has grown so much in two months. There's just a few weeks to go now, and we have so much to look forward to.

After another round of media interviews, I say goodbye to the guys. We have shared so much over the past few weeks, and I suppose our achievement means that, as long as we live, there will always be some kind of special bond between us.

The M25 is busy on a cold Tuesday morning four weeks before Christmas. I turn on BBC Radio Five Live, and hear an interview with Martin Johnson. 'People should recognise the contribution of the guys who have worked so hard and achieved so much but didn't get on the field in the final,' the captain says.

'Somebody like Kyran Bracken sat on the bench, but he was one of our stars in the match against South Africa.'

I smile.

Thanks, Johnno. Thanks, Clive.

Thanks, everyone. It's been great.

CHAPTER FIVE

Monday, 8 December 2003
THE STREETS OF LONDON

Nobody wanted the Webb Ellis Cup. We had worked so hard to win this thing, but none of the guys would touch it.

Why? Well, it was embarrassing. We had won the World Cup in what is probably the ultimate team sport, and it just felt wrong to carry the trophy as if you'd done it all on your own. This sentiment spread through the squad to a point where, every time we had to appear with the cup, nobody wanted to hold it. Through all the World Cup celebration events that took place towards the end of 2003 and into 2004, you could be sure the only reason any player was carrying the trophy was that he'd somehow got stuck with it and nobody would take it off him. This was the case when we stood on the open double-decker bus that carried us on a victory parade through London on Monday, 8 December 2003. Clive wasn't keen on going near the cup under any circumstances, Johnno generally looked the other way and Jonny stood at the opposite end of the bus.

Nonetheless, it was a great day, and we felt the full force of what winning a major team cup for the first time since

1966 meant to so many English people. After thirty-seven years of hurt, to paraphrase the football song, Webb Ellis was finally gleaming.

Most of the England guys had been allowed to rest for a week or so after getting home from Australia, but we were then expected back at the day job, playing for the clubs who pay our salaries, and the normal routine seemed to resume quite quickly.

Was that it? Perhaps a sense of anticlimax was inevitable as each of us contemplated a lifetime spent looking back on what we had achieved together in 2003. At least we could still look forward to the big day of celebrations in London.

An unprecedented series of events was planned to take place on a freezing, damp Monday morning in December and, even after our amazing welcome at Heathrow, some of us doubted whether the street parade would be a success. Anyway, we were determined to enjoy ourselves and, as the guys gathered at a West End hotel early in the morning, everyone was in high spirits. We had shared so much as a squad and, even though our job was done, we were still a squad. I daresay we will always be a squad.

Dress code was our grey World Cup suits, although they had been designed for the Australian summer rather than sub-zero London in the depths of winter. I reckoned we would freeze on top of the bus but, in the event, the sights and sounds of a genuinely amazing day kept us all more than warm.

There were a decent number of people milling around when we got on board the bus outside the hotel in Park Lane, but none of us will forget the sight that confronted us as we turned the corner at Marble Arch and looked down Oxford Street: just a mass of people, packing the pavements, waving out of windows, perched on street lights, every-where, all shouting and cheering. I was amazed. Many of us felt as if we were playing some kind of surreal game where ordinary people are treated like superstars for a day. This kind of hysteria was completely new to us, but the guys were lapping it all up and enjoying every minute.

There was still the issue of who would hold the trophy, and we agreed to operate a rota where each of the players would take a turn with the cup at the front of the bus, all except Jonny, who was still determined to keep out of the limelight at the back. He was having to work hard. Most of the banners declared undying love for him and at one point I had to pull him back to prevent him being trapped in a photograph with two topless girls.

This amazing flood of noise and people flowed continu-ously all the way down Oxford Street, right into Regent Street, on through Piccadilly Circus and into Trafalgar Square, where our bus came to a halt for some speeches and fireworks. A few supporters braved the bitter cold and began splashing around in the fountains, but nobody seemed to mind. I later read there had been more than a million people lining the route, and not a single arrest.

Next stop, Buckingham Palace. Together with our wives and girlfriends, we arrived by bus and were ushered into a large room to wait for the Queen. Some of the guys couldn't resist having a go at Mike Tindall, asking if he would mind introducing them to his future in-laws. Our centre was rumoured to have become a close friend of Zara Phillips, Princess Anne's daughter, but he grinned, took all the banter in good heart and looked a little nervous.

We all fell silent when a huge pair of oak doors swung open and we turned to see not the monarch but four or five corgis and other dogs scamper into the room. Queen Elizabeth II followed and, looking very relaxed, spent quite a while talking to the players before sitting with us for a photograph, made special by a few of her dogs running around in the foreground. She also chatted to some of the wives, including Victoria, putting everyone at ease.

We were then whisked straight from the Palace to Downing Street, where the Prime Minister hosted an official reception for us at No. 10. Tony Blair was the perfect host, but most of us were excited to see Gordon Brown there as well. Somebody had told us how the England football players that won the 1966 World Cup were given tax exemption on the money they earned as a result, and we were eager to hear from the present Chancellor of the Exchequer whether a similar deal might not seem appropriate for us.

Unsure of how to raise the subject, some of the guys thought it would be a good idea to stand in the vicinity of Mr Brown and just say the word 'tax', vaguely concealed in a cough. This barrage of mumbling and coughing continued for twenty minutes or so and, while it was really funny to watch, it failed completely.

This was obviously not a time for subtlety, so we organised a quick game of spoof among the players and agreed the loser would approach the notoriously prudent Chancellor and ask him directly about tax. Mike Tindall lost and, as we hovered in the background, he duly walked up and posed the question. Gordon Brown listened, laughed out loud and carried on. We might have beaten the best in world rugby, but we were getting no change from him.

An unforgettable day ended with a special dinner for all the Saracens players, from five different countries, who had played at the World Cup. Everybody we met, from the

Queen and the Prime Minister to the people lining the streets and the guests at the dinner, seemed so proud of what he had achieved, so excited, so full of compliments and praise. It just didn't stop.

The following afternoon, I was one of four World Cup players asked to parade the trophy around the field at Twickenham before the Varsity Match. Joe Worsley was another, but he got stitched up when the three of us persuaded him to be the first one to hold the cup as we began the lap of honour. We simply refused to take it off him. Every time he tried to pass it on, we turned away and waved at the crowd. As we laughed, Joe ended up carrying it the whole way round. He won't get caught out again.

I received a message soon after the match, telling me that Victoria had been admitted to hospital. She wasn't due for another two weeks and as I rushed to get there I didn't think our first child was quite ready to be born. I was wrong. I arrived to find Victoria four centimetres dilated. Things were clearly moving. As I stood by her bed, wanting to be helpful and constructive and inevitably being as helpless and hopeless as every prospective father, I looked at my wife and, I clearly remember, suddenly felt overwhelmed by a sense of having been so lucky.

What would have happened if I hadn't made that last-minute decision to go to the Leopard Lounge in London on New Year's Day in 1999? What would have happened if Fran, then Andy Gomarsall's girlfriend and later his wife, had not introduced me to a beautiful law student? What would have happened if we hadn't fallen in love and got married in St Alban's on 22 July 2001? What would have happened if Victoria hadn't been there for me ever since, giving me unconditional support when I needed it most?

What if? It didn't matter. Yes, I had been lucky, but the fact was that there we were together, in this neat hospital room, ready to be transformed from a young couple into a family. If one chapter of our lives was coming to a close, then it was also true that I could not wait to turn the page and start the next.

Through so many eager, exhilarated discussions, I had always told Victoria that I would be very happy if our first child turned out to be a daughter. It was the truth, but I also didn't want my wife to feel under any pressure to produce the 'son and heir'. The gender of our baby seemed completely unimportant to me.

Charlie, our son, was born later that night. I stood there and watched him arrive in our world and, in that moment, found myself feeling as profoundly happy as I have ever felt.

Being picked for England Schools, playing in an unforgettable Bristol team, making my debut in an England team that beat the All Blacks at Twickenham, helping Saracens to win the first trophy in their history, earning my fiftieth international cap, even winning the World Cup – everything that I had always thought so important almost immediately seemed so insignificant in comparison with the reality of us . . . of me, Victoria and Charlie.

I don't want to sound like a guest on daytime television, and I don't need Oprah or even Jerry Springer to put a caring hand on my shoulder, but Charlie's birth changed my life.

How?

It put rugby into perspective.

For so many years, people had looked at Kyran Bracken and seen a cheerful guy, playing for his club, playing for England, being part of everything, always having a laugh, having a drink, loving the banter, training hard, just loving the rugby life. They didn't see the half of it. They didn't see how the intense, sustained pressure of playing sport at the highest level had started to cause real physical symptoms: the unexplained bouts of nausea, the sleeplessness and the adrenaline rushes.

Beyond my family and closest friends, nobody knew when I reached a stage where I didn't believe I could get to sleep unless there was absolute silence and I was on my own. Nobody saw me on the night when I couldn't sleep in my own hotel room, left my roomie alone and wandered around until I finally got some rest on a spare bed in the room we used for physiotherapy.

And they didn't see me when I lay in bed before an important Saracens game and convinced myself I couldn't sleep because I could hear the whirring sound of the hotel's generator. It was after eleven o'clock, but I went down to reception and asked the night manager to give me another room. He was able to help, so I went back upstairs, packed my suitcase and moved. That was a nuisance, but I thought I could still hear the same noise and I still couldn't get to sleep so, around two in the morning, I went back to reception and asked for another room. They obliged again, I packed my suitcase again, moved again and only then slept in what was my third different bed of the night.

People in the game didn't see how the pressure had started to affect me. They didn't see how twelve years of trying to do my best, of being judged, of being selected, dropped, picked again, dropped again, of worrying what newspapers and coaches thought about me, of living under a spotlight, had taken its toll.

I suppose I was the classic swan, happy and serene above the surface but, beneath, paddling like crazy to stay afloat;

and while it was all going on I didn't connect any of my symptoms with playing top-class sport. When something felt wrong, I simply went to see a doctor or a specialist, often without success.

Britt Tajet-Foxell, my sports psychologist, helped me start to understand what was happening to me, and my situation has eased under her guidance, but the amazing effect of Charlie's birth on my life has been to switch on the auto-focus. All of a sudden, I can see what's truly important, and it's not what a reporter writes about my performance, and it's not even the result of England's next international. In truth, and quite literally in my case, these things are not worth losing sleep over. It doesn't mean I'm not committed, or I don't try, or that I somehow don't care as much. I just have a better perspective. Nowadays, by and large, the only thing that keeps us awake at night is Charlie, needing to be fed, needing his nappy changed or just needing some attention. That's no problem.

Towards the end of 2003, I was selected in the England squad for the game against the Barbarians at Twickenham and, although I was put on the bench behind Gommers, I was looking forward to the occasion not only because it was billed as the homecoming of the new world champions but also because I was going to receive an award to mark my fifty international caps.

The RFU tend to get things exactly right on these occasions, and I was touched by the presentation of a mounted silver cap. Jonny also got one at the same time, because he had reached the same milestone as me and, earlier in the year, Jason Leonard had got a gold cap to recognise his 100 caps. Players appreciate such gestures. In recent months, for example, the RFU has sent each of the World Cup players an engraved solid silver plate, a specially designed England jersey and other gifts. I detect Clive's hand in all of this but if the officials are trying to reaffirm pride and encourage commitment, that's exactly what they achieve.

In any case, as the Baabaas game ran its course, I sat there on the bench and started to wonder whether it could turn out to be the last time I wore an England jersey at Twickenham, even though this game didn't count as a full international. There was not long to go and, as usual, Clive had bounced down from his normal seat in the west stand to sit beside the substitutes.

He tapped me on the shoulder. 'KB,' the coach said, 'thanks for everything you have done over the years.'

That was odd, I thought to myself. Why has he said that? Was he trying to give me a hint? Is he saying I should jump before I get pushed out of the England set-up? I didn't know, and I didn't feel any need to seek clarification. If that's what the coach had in mind, then he was thinking along the same lines as me.

Our World Cup celebrations continued into the New Year, with the trophy being paraded at club grounds, more lunches, dinners and formal occasions, and it was entirely predictable that this huge party should be followed by a huge hangover.

Into January and February 2004, most of the England players found themselves physically and mentally exhausted. It was an odd feeling for me, unlike anything I had known before. I was beginning to dread training and scarcely looked forward to matches. We had been training and playing at high intensity, without a decent break, for almost two years. The batteries were flat.

Several members of the World Cup squad, like Jonny,

Lewis Moody and Iain Balshaw, suffered serious injuries, and others, like me, lost form. Catty was battling at Bath, and subsequently moved to London Irish. Daws struggled at Northampton, and later switched to Wasps. I wasn't satisfied with my performances for Saracens, but the club was understanding and sympathetic.

Something clearly needed to be done. Retiring completely was not an option, because I still wanted to achieve great things with Saracens, but I decided the best way of prolonging that club career was to retire from international rugby. Victoria and I discussed the pros and cons, and agreed. After more than ten years in the England set-up, after helping the team to win forty out of fifty-one internationals, after winning the World Cup, what was left?

Money? Perhaps, but that has never been a reason for me to play rugby. I have never worked harder in my career than I did to earn my first cap, and that was for nothing. Status and fame? Well, I won't pretend I didn't enjoy the attention earlier in my career but the remnants of that profile had become a hassle. Would I miss the buzz? Hand on heart, not really. I'd had enough.

Clive had included me in a preliminary training squad for the 2004 Six Nations campaign, and he also declared every player had to make themselves available for the summer tour to New Zealand and Australia. The mere mention of yet another trip to the opposite end of the world filled me with horror, but I still turned up to the England training camp, probably out of habit. I remember thinking to myself, what the hell am I still doing here?

Johnno had already retired from the international game, so it seemed sensible to phone him for a chat and tell him what I felt. He was great, as usual, explaining that it was a very personal thing but adding I should do what my heart said. If you just don't want it any more, the ex-captain told me, bow out. I phoned Clive the very next day and informed him of my decision.

'You shouldn't do that,' the coach told me. 'Nobody can retire from international rugby. It's something that just happens. I didn't retire from the England team, and neither should you.'

'What about Johnno?' I asked.

'That was different,' he said.

He then told me I would not be named in the England squad to start the Six Nations but added that, if my form for Saracens was good, I would be considered for subsequent matches. I told him to count me out. OK, he replied, but asked me not to make any statement until after he had announced the England squad.

I gave him that assurance, more out of loyalty than anything else, but I felt annoyed because that sequence of events was going to make my retirement look like a reaction to being left out of the squad, which it wasn't. I had wanted to end my international career on my terms, but was denied that opportunity.

So, once more, I had to suffer the hurt and indignity of being dropped by England. It doesn't get any easier. I hated it the first time in 1994, and I hated it the last time as well. I would love to be able to say I didn't care any more, but I did. More than anything, I loathe that feeling of not being good enough.

Maybe it has been precisely because I hate it so much that, all through my career, I have fought my way back. Looking back over the past decade, nothing matters to me quite so much as the fact that, whenever I have been dropped, I have always fought back and regained my place in the team. So many players come and go, but I have managed to go and keep coming back.

Two weeks later, spending some time at my parents' home in Jersey, I talked over things with my family, especially Louise who has always been 100 per cent supportive and who knows me as well as anyone. She told me to do what made me happy. I decided I would announce my decision, no matter what anyone else said. I phoned Clive and made sure he heard the news first. He was very understanding, thanking me for my efforts again, and wishing me all the best. My next call was to the local news office at Jersey TV, because I wanted them to have the exclusive story of my decision. It just felt right to make the announcement where my family was based.

The response was reassuring. People called, asking me for my reasons, and Clive and my team-mates said some kind things in the papers, about me as a player and a person. It was a good decision, and I haven't regretted it for a moment.

Perhaps the same sense of fatigue that prompted me to retire from international rugby was the main reason for England's defeats to Ireland and France in the 2004 Six Nations, and the subsequent losses to the All Blacks and Australia on the summer tour. We were missing several key players for various reasons, and I'm sure the setbacks will prove a temporary blip, but some good will come of this run of defeats if it can demonstrate to the officials that we are being asked to play too much rugby.

My view is that a modern professional should have to play no more than thirty matches per season, instead of the thirty-eight or forty we are currently playing, and that he should have a mandatory eleven-week off-season. I realise there are commercial demands involved, but the top players are the game's prize assets, and it is only common sense for everyone involved – the RFU, the clubs, the England squad, the sponsors and the broadcasters – that those assets are protected, not treated like battery hens.

The future of the England team seems uncertain. Clive had told the players that his burning ambition was to win another World Cup with England, but what we didn't realise at the time was that he meant with a different-shaped ball. So, the guys were genuinely surprised when the head coach resigned at the start of September 2004, saying that he would concentrate on preparing the Lions for their tour to New Zealand in 2005. After that, it seems he will make a serious attempt to switch codes and be successful in football. If he pursues this ambition, it will be interesting to see how far he goes. Given his experience and determination, I wouldn't be surprised if Clive bridges the gap and embarks on a second career.

For now, I am content to focus all my energies on helping my club realise its vast potential. Saracens have promised so much and delivered so little in recent times, but I believe the combination of talented coaches, Rod Kafer, Mike Ford and Steve Diamond, and an exciting blend of youth and exper-ience will bring success. Hopefully, there will be more medals to store away alongside the one I received in Sydney on my thirty-second birthday.

At least I'll always have that. Or maybe not. Towards the end of 2003, I actually lost my World Cup winner's medal. Victoria and I looked everywhere but couldn't find it and I began to enquire if it was possible to organise a replacement.

Then, one night, while writing this book in my study, I heard the sound of Charlie crying in his room. I went

upstairs and tried to comfort him. All of sudden, I remembered how I had got back late at night from a World
Cup function and, while giving him a bottle, had put the
medal away in his nappy drawer.

A quick rummage uncovered the single object that, I
suppose, will always be the symbol of a fantastic England
career that is past. A quick glance at Charlie, my baby son,
reminded me how much our family can look forward to the
future that lies ahead.

APPENDIX A: LIST OF INTERNATIONAL APPEARANCES

CAP	DATE	TOURNAMENT	OPPONENTS
1	27 November 1993	F	New Zealand
2	5 February 1994	FN	Scotland
3	19 February 1994	FN	Ireland
4	10 December 1994	F	Canada
5	21 January 1995	FN	Ireland
6	4 February 1995	FN	France
7	18 February 1995	FN	Wales
8	18 March 1995	FN	Scotland
9	31 May 1995	WC	Italy
10	4 June 1995	WC	Western Samoa
11	18 November 1995	F	South Africa
12	23 November 1996	F	Italy
13	31 May 1997	F	Argentina
14	7 June 1997	F	Argentina
15	15 November 1997	F	Australia
16	22 November 1997	F	New Zealand
17	6 December 1997	F	New Zealand
18	8 February 1998	FN	France
19	21 February 1998	FN	Wales
20	20 February 1999	FN	Scotland
21	6 March 1999	FN	Ireland
22	20 March 1999	FN	France
23	26 June 1999	F	Australia
24	17 June 2000	F	South Africa
25	24 June 2000	F	South Africa
26	18 November 2000	F	Australia
27	17 February 2001	SN	Italy

VENUE	RESULT	REPLACEMENT/TRY
Twickenham	W 15–9	-
Edinburgh	W 15–14	-
Twickenham	L 12–13	-
Twickenham	W 60–19	One Try
Dublin	W 20–8	-
Twickenham	W 31–10	-
Cardiff	W 23–9	-
Twickenham	W 24–12	-
Durban	W 27–20	-
Durban	W 44–22	-
Twickenham	L 24–14	-
Twickenham	W 54–21	Replacement
Buenos Aires	W 46–20	-
Buenos Aires	L 33–13	-
Twickenham	D 15–15	-
Old Trafford	L 25–8	-
Twickenham	D 26–26	-
Paris	L 24–17	-
Twickenham	W 60–26	One Try
Twickenham	W 24–21	Replacement
Dublin	W 27–15	-
Twickenham	W 21–10	-
Sydney	L 22–15	-
Pretoria	L 18–13	-
Bloemfontein	W 27–22	-
Twickenham	W 22–19	-
Cardiff	W 80–23	Replacement

CAP	DATE	TOURNAMENT	OPPONENTS
28	3 March 2001	SN	Scotland
29	7 April 2001	SN	France
30	2 June 2001	F	Canada
31	9 June 2001	F	Canada
32	16 June 2001	F	USA
33	20 October 2001	SN	Ireland
34	10 November 2001	F	Australia
35	17 November 2001	F	Romania
36	24 November 2001	F	South Africa
37	2 February 2002	SN	Scotland
38	16 February 2002	SN	Ireland
39	2 March 2002	SN	France
40	23 March 2002	SN	Wales
41	7 April 2002	SN	Italy
42	22 February 2003	SN	Wales
43	9 March 2003	SN	Italy
44	30 March 2003	SN	Ireland
45	14 June 2003	F	New Zealand
46	21 June 2003	F	Australia
47	6 September 2003	F	France
48	18 October 2003	WC	South Africa
49	2 November 2003	WC	Uruguay
50	9 November 2003	WC	Wales
51	16 November 2003	WC	France

F   Friendly   WC   World Cup
FN   Five Nations   SN   Six Nations

VENUE	RESULT	REPLACEMENT/TRY
Twickenham	W 43–3	Replacement
Twickenham	W 48–19	Replacement
Markham	W 22–10	One Try
Burnaby	W 59–20	-
San Francisco	W 48–19	-
Dublin	L 20–14	Replacement
Twickenham	W 21–15	-
Twickenham	W 134–0	Replacement
Twickenham	W 29–9	-
Edinburgh	W 29–3	-
Twickenham	W 45–11	-
Paris	L 20–15	-
Twickenham	W 50–10	-
Rome	W 45–9	-
Cardiff	W 26–9	-
Twickenham	W 40–5	Replacement
Dublin	W 42–6	Replacement
Wellington	W 15–13	-
Melbourne	W 25–14	-
Twickenham	W 45–14	-
Perth	W 25–6	-
Brisbane	W 111–13	Replacement
Brisbane	W 28–17	Replacement
Sydney	W 24–7	Replacement

Overall Career Record v Other Nations

Opponents	Played	Won	Drawn	Lost
Argentina	2	1	0	1
Australia	5	3	1	1
Canada	3	3	0	0
France	7	5	0	2
Ireland	6	4	0	2
Italy	5	5	0	0
New Zealand	4	2	1	1
Romania	1	1	0	0
Scotland	5	5	0	0
South Africa	5	3	0	2
Uruguay	1	1	0	0
USA	1	1	0	0
Wales	5	5	0	0
Western Samoa	1	1	0	0
Total	51	40	2	9

APPENDIX B:
DREAM TEAMS

Almost since the day William Webb Ellis picked up the football and ran, rugby players have passed many happy hours selecting a wide variety of different teams. Travelling to and from matches, waiting at airports, sitting around after training, whenever, the suggestion to choose a team usually gets a positive response.

So I have indulged myself by compiling a couple of all-time selections: first, my Dream Team, which is not my World XV but is chosen only from those who have been my team-mates; second, a Tough XV, who you'd always want on your side. I also thought of choosing a Bald XV, because that's one side from which I will never get dropped.

DREAM XV

Tighthead prop:	Roberto Grau
Hooker:	Mark Regan
Loosehead prop:	Cobus Visagie
Second row:	Martin Johnson (captain)
Second row:	Simon Shaw
Flanker:	Richard Hill
Flanker:	Derek Eves
No. 8:	Lawrence Dallaglio
Scrum-half:	——
Fly-half:	Jonny Wilkinson
Left wing:	Jason Robinson
Centre:	Philippe Sella
Centre:	Will Carling
Right wing:	Ben Cohen
Full-back:	Thomas Castaignède
Head coach:	*Clive Woodward*

TOUGH XV

Tighthead prop:	Richard Loe
Hooker:	Sean Fitzpatrick
Loosehead prop:	Darren Garforth
Second row:	Garath Archer
Second row:	Martin Johnson
Flanker:	Francois Pienaar
Flanker:	Andre Venter
No. 8:	Buck Shelford
Scrum-half:	Richard Hill
Fly-half:	Henry Honiball
Left wing:	Freddie Tuilagi
Centre:	Brendan Venter
Centre:	Frank Bunce
Right wing:	Brian Lima
Full-back:	Mike Umaga

INDEX